The Key to Faith

Meditations on the Liturgical Year

Adolf Adam

Translated by Patrick Madigan, S.J.

A Liturgical Press Book

THE LITURGICAL PRESS
Collegeville, Minnesota

Cover design by David Manahan, O.S.B. Line art illustrations by Getrud Mueller Nelson.

The Key to Faith: Meditations on the Liturgical Year is the authorized English translation of *Das Kirchenjahr: Schlüssel zum Glauben, Betrachtungen,* copyright © by Verlag Herder, Freiburg im Breisgau, 1990. The publisher of this English edition has adapted the liturgical texts and commentary to conform to the current official usage in the United States.

Scripture quotations are from the New Revised Standard Version Bible, Catholic edition, © 1989 by the Division of Christian Education of the National Council of Churches of Christ in the U.S.A. Used by permission. All rights reserved.

Excerpts are also taken from the New American Bible, © 1991, 1986, 1970 by the Confraternity of Christian Doctrine, 3211 Fourth Street N.E., Washington, DC 20017-1194 and are used by permission of the copyright holder. All rights reserved.

Excerpts from the English translation of *Lectionary for Mass* © 1969, 1981, International Committee on English in the Liturgy, Inc. (ICEL); excerpts from the English translation of *The Roman Missal* © 1973, ICEL. All rights reserved.

1   2   3   4   5   6   7   8

Library of Congress Cataloging-in-Publication Data

Adam, Adolf, 1912–
    [Kirchenjahr. English]
    The key to faith : meditations on the liturgical year / Adolf Adam ; translated by Patrick Madigan.
        p.   cm.
    Includes bibliographical references and index.
    ISBN 0-8146-2449-9 (alk. paper)
    1. Church year meditations.   I. Title.
BX2170.C55A2313   1998
    242'.3—dc21   97-51478
                                                                      CIP

In memory of

Hanne-Lore Czaja

September 21, 1935—August 1, 1989

Editor at Herder Verlag

and

Vera Spaeth

March 4, 1921—September 9, 1988

Household Manager

with gratitude and esteem

CONTENTS

Solemnities of the Lord in Ordinary Time

A Selection from the Proper of the Saints

FOREWORD

There have been times and places where the festivals of the church year were almost the only means of transmitting the faith. This historical precedent may serve as a worthwhile suggestion for our own period, in which the struggle to pass the faith on has become ever more difficult, a time, indeed, in which the Christian message seems to be embroiled in "a fight to the death" (Newman). Yet we may still discover in the liturgical year the fullness of the Christian proclamation of salvation garbed in a vivid and richly symbolic vesture.

Unfortunately, for many people the proverb "you can't love what you don't know" seems only too true. One does not have to view the world through dark glasses to suspect that knowledge of the church year and its faith content persists today only in a vestigial way and on a superficial level. In this situation the present book seeks to provide some aid both for deepening one's own faith as well as for passing it on to others.

My intention has been to convey the wealth of meaning and faith of the liturgical year in accessible language. For this purpose I have chosen the following method: for each feast day I provide a liturgical guide (giving the history of the feast and the specifics of its celebration); there follows a spiritual reflection that expands the meaning of the feast and interprets its significance for our contemporary world; finally the reflections are completed by a text to inspire further meditation.

Mainz, Easter 1990

Adolf Adam

The Christmas Cycle

ADVENT

General Introduction

In the West, in a process similar to the celebration of Easter, the celebration of Christmas developed a period of preparation. The historical process took place differently in Spain and Gaul than it did at Rome. In Gaul, under the influence of Irish missionaries, Advent took on a penitential character expressed in the dropping of the Gloria and alleluia from the Mass and the *Te Deum* from the Divine Office, and in the use of violet vestments at Mass. In the twelfth century some of these elements even made their way into the Roman liturgy, which, however, through its maintenance of the alleluia made it clear that it did not regard Advent as truly a period of penance. As for the length of the season of Advent, the Roman solution of four Sundays eventually established itself almost everywhere. (To this day the Milanese rite contains seven Sundays for Advent.)

The *General Roman Calendar* (= GRC, 1969) sees the significance of Advent both as a time of preparation for the solemnity of the Lord's birth and as an anticipation of his return at the end of time. "It is thus a season of joyful and spiritual expectation." (*GRC* 39)

Liturgically there is a distinction between two phases of Advent. The first runs until December 16 and is oriented principally toward the return of Christ at the end of time. In the days from December 17 to 24 Advent is characterized more by the anticipation of Christmas, which comes to expression primarily in the scriptural readings chosen for the Mass. It is during this second phase that the famous "O antiphons" embellish the Magnificat during the Liturgy of the Hours, and simultaneously serve as the alleluia during the celebration of Mass.

If December 24 falls on a Sunday, the liturgy of the Vigil of Christmas is not celebrated. It is replaced by that of the Fourth Sunday of Advent.

The new Roman Missal, in contrast to its predecessor, contains two Prefaces exclusively for Advent. The German Missal has added three more, certainly a sizable enrichment for the Advent liturgy.

The German Missal provides directly above each Preface a short summary of its content; these suggest, in different ways, the variety of Advent perspectives:

I   The twofold coming of Christ
II   Waiting for the Lord, in history and today
III The gifts of the Lord who is approaching
IV   The sin of Adam and the grace of Christ
V   The Lord is near

The variety of customs associated with the Advent season is explained partly by the character of the season as an anticipation of Christmas, and partly as a vestige of pre-Christian (Germanic) practices linked with the winter solstice.

Even if Advent is not properly a penitential season, it should still be viewed as a quiet and reflective period. For that reason it is regrettable that today these weeks are often reduced to nothing more than an excuse for parties. It is therefore all the more important to stress the season's authentic meaning and religious richness, which provide an occasion not only for worship services, but also for religious instruction, community catechesis, and other pastoral projects.

First Sunday of Advent

LITURGICAL GUIDE

In this and the following introductions we are concerned only with the Sunday Mass celebration, not with the Liturgy of the Hours, even though the latter is also an important part of the liturgy as a whole. Regarding the celebration of the Mass on the four Sundays of Advent, it should be noted that their respective selections in the three liturgical cycles (year A = Matthew; year B = Mark; year C = Luke) are all the same, with the exception of the Old Testament readings, the responsorial psalms, and occasionally also the alleluia verses.

What is decisive for the character of the Mass celebration is the Gospel for that week. On the first Sunday of Advent the Gospel speaks of the return of the Lord in power and splendor. This will take place suddenly and unexpectedly; no one knows the day or the hour. For that reason all the pericopes contain the counsel to remain wakeful and watchful.

The Old Testament readings are taken from the prophets Isaiah and Jeremiah. In year A they speak of the messianic reign of peace toward which all nations will stream. They will turn their swords into plowshares and their spears into pruning hooks. The pericope in B contains the imploring plea for the coming of the Lord: "Oh, that you would rend the heavens and come down!" Year C gives us the promise concerning the upright son of David.

The New Testament readings come from a variety of the Pauline epistles. All direct our gaze toward the second coming of Christ: "It is now the hour for you to wake from sleep" (A: Rom 13:11); Christ will "strengthen you to the end, so that you will be blameless on the day of our Lord Jesus Christ" (B: 1 Cor 1:8); "May the Lord increase you . . . making [your hearts] blameless and holy . . . at the coming of our Lord Jesus with all his holy ones" (C: 1 Thess 3:12-13). Advent petitions in various forms are also contained in the opening prayer, the prayer over the gifts, and the concluding prayer.

SPIRITUAL REFLECTION

A seller who puts a false label on a product is liable to be taken to court; this has been made clear in recent years by many lawsuits. And this is as it should be. A person who, responding to the reputation of a brand name, puts out good money for what should be a top-of-the-line product, only to receive cleverly concealed inferior goods, has a right to feel deceived and indignant.

In our time, Advent is being similarly mislabeled; however, very few seem to be upset about it. The sophisticated methods of advertising, the "hidden persuaders" as a well-known book once put it, denature it into a time of frenetic gift buying. Streets and malls are decorated with Christmas trees radiant with ornaments; main streets are garlanded overhead with stars blinking on and off; in the stores the personnel are dressed to look like Santa's helpers; weeks before Christmas, businesses and civic organizations hold their annual "Christmas parties," with gift-giving and good cheer all around. Glasses clink and toasts are drunk to the Christmas spirit, to good will towards all, to the family celebration, to peace. That this happens to be the occasion of somebody's birthday, and who that somebody is who is having a birthday—these are things that few people dare to mention.

Anyone who really understands Advent must regard all this as mislabeling, deception, advertising something under false pretenses. Here,

Upon those who are exhausted from the frantic activity before
    Christmas,
in our midst, in our town, in the world:
give them peace and strength
and a quiet, deep faith in yourself.

Upon those who become depressed and irritable during this season:
stand by them like a protecting wall:
impart new strength to their faith
and a fresh, new gleam to their hope and love.

And upon all who are disappointed and confused:
bring them home; have compassion on them all;
help them discover new friends and a renewed energy.

We also pray for justice and peace
and freedom for the whole earth:
O Lord, come to the aid of all people and
guide them to your salvation!

O Lord, be our shelter!
Be our house, be our peace!
In every day, in every night.
Through Christ, our Lord.

Bernhard Welte[1]

Second Sunday of Advent

LITURGICAL GUIDE

The Advent promises, exhortation, and a joyous anticipation distinguish this Sunday and are concentrated in the opening verse, which draws on words from the prophet Isaiah:

> People of Zion, the Lord will come to save all nations, and your hearts
> will exult to hear his majestic voice.

All three Gospel selections, from the synoptic authors, contain the preaching of repentance by John the Baptist, the one who came before and prepared the way. "Reform your lives! The reign of God is at hand" (Matt 3:2); he cried, "proclaiming a baptism of repentance which led to the forgiveness of sins" (Mark 1:4; similarly Luke 3:3). All the evangelists see in this preaching of repentance the fulfillment of what Isaiah had prophesied: "A voice cries out: in the wilderness prepare the way of the Lord, make straight in the desert a highway for our God" (Isa 40:3).

The Old Testament reading for year A promises the Messiah as the shoot from the "stump of Jesse" and paints his kingdom in glowing colors. In the pericopes for years B and C, the return of the people of God from exile in Babylon is used as an inspiring simile for the completion of salvation that the Messiah will realize (Isa 40:1-5, 9-11, and Bar 5:1-9).

In the readings from the New Testament, Christ is proclaimed as the bearer of universal salvation (A: Rom 15:4-9); he will bring down a new heaven and a new earth, in which justice will be at home (B: 2 Peter 3:8-14); in anticipation of this "day of Christ Jesus" we should have a "clear conscience and blameless conduct" and be "rich in the harvest of justice" (C: Phil 1:4-6, 8-11). The opening prayer summarizes these thoughts and admonitions when it prays God to "remove the things that hinder us from receiving Christ with joy."

SPIRITUAL REFLECTION

The Gospels for the Masses of the second and third Sundays of Advent in all three cycles describe the activities of John the Baptist. Also, in the Gospel selections for the weekdays from Thursday of the second week of Advent to December 16, the topic is the significance of the Baptist. For that reason he is correctly termed the preacher of Advent.

Already at the circumcision of the infant John his father Zechariah, inspired by the Holy Spirit, had prophesied that this child would go before the Lord as the "prophet of the Most High" and would prepare the way for him (Luke 1:76). The evangelists all see in his appearance the fulfillment of the saying of Isaiah the prophet. As Luke's gospel reads:

> . . . as it is written in the book
> of the words of the prophet Isaiah:
> "The voice of one crying out in the wilderness:
> Prepare the way of the Lord,
> make his paths straight.
> Every valley shall be filled,
> and every mountain and hill shall be made low,

and the crooked shall be made straight,
and the rough ways made smooth;
and all flesh shall see the salvation of God" (Luke 3:4-6).

As the word of God reached John in the desert, he went "into all the region around the Jordan, proclaiming a baptism of repentance for the forgiveness of sins" (Luke 3:3). Much of what John proclaimed at that time merits attention today as well.

His first major theme is: Reflect, repent, convert! In every age people fall prey to the temptation to overturn the proper order of values. What is important is degraded to a minor matter, what is minor or even wrong is raised to a principal theme, the central issue of one's life. It can be greed, of which the poet says: "Strive after gold, for everything indeed depends on gold" (Goethe). It can be ambition with its exhibitionistic and ruthless careerism. It can be quarrelsomeness and the insistence on always being right, or envy and a desire to dominate, or the unmastered desire for pleasure that Paul at one point so powerfully describes: "their god is the belly" (Phil 3:19). These are all products of egoism, which places one's own self in the center and degenerates into idolatry. The great Thomas Aquinas states at one point that the cause of all sin is egoism. Once it has taken over a person, that person's heart remains closed to the love of God and neighbor. It digs a deep chasm, an "abyss" between God and the person; it separates us from God; egoism becomes an equivalent word for sin.

John sees this clearly and therefore calls for reflection: Admit your offense, confess your sin and let yourself be cleansed. As a symbol of such purification he offers a baptism of repentance in the Jordan.

John's preaching of repentance was directed at distinct groups of people, and thereby took on a variety of forms. He reproaches the Pharisees and Sadducees for their conceit and self-righteousness. Those who view themselves as holy are light-years away from true holiness. Nor is the invocation of an illustrious paternity of any use: If you mean to imply that your descent from Abraham is already enough for your salvation, I have this to say to you: from these very stones God can raise up new children of Abraham. God is in no way dependent on you (cf. Luke 3:8).

When the simple people then begin to ask him what they should do, he refers them to specific types of love of neighbor: "Whoever has two coats must share with anyone who has none; and whoever has food must do likewise" (Luke 3:11). To the tax collectors, whose chief vice was apparently avarice, and as a consequence the cheating of travelers, he gives the advice: "Collect no more than the amount prescribed for you" (Luke 3:13). Translated into a modern idiom this means: Do not raise your prices too high, be honest in your bills, do not take advantage of your favored position to exploit the customers! Soldiers as well, in those times hardly honest citizens in uniform, but rather feared extorters, came to him for advice. His answer: "Do not extort money from anyone by threats or false accusation, and be satisfied with your wages" (Luke 3:14).

How would he respond if one of us asked him the question "What can, what should I do to prepare a way for the Lord in my life?" Would not John's answer to us also be "reflect and revise your thinking"? Indeed, self-knowledge is the first step toward self-improvement. But if you truly know yourself, you will recognize your faults and deficiencies, which then should be removed.

The second major theme of John's preaching is his witness for Jesus as the Messiah sent from God. When many people asked John whether he himself was not the Messiah (or "Christ"), he answered clearly: "I am not the Messiah . . . I am the voice of one crying out in the wilderness, 'Make straight the way of the Lord'" (John 1:20-23). "The one who is more powerful than I is coming after me; I am not worthy to stoop down and untie the thong of his sandals. I have baptized you with water; but he will baptize you with the Holy Spirit" (Mark 1:7-8). "Among you stands one whom you do not know, the one who is coming after me . . . Here is the Lamb of God who takes away the sin of the world! This is he of whom I said, 'After me comes a man who ranks ahead of me because he was before me' . . . I myself have seen and have testified that this is the Son of God" (John 1:26-34).

John experiences no envy of Jesus when his disciples tell him that Jesus is attracting greater numbers than he is. Selflessly he answers: "He must increase, but I must decrease" (John 3:30).

What strengthens John's credibility in the eyes of the people is his personal unpretentiousness in matters of food and clothing, as well as his fearless outspokenness in the name of justice and righteousness, which we know led also to his martyr's death at the hands of Herod.

We thus meet in John a persuasive preacher of Advent. He makes clear that the royal Messiah will enter only where people have torn down the various barriers around their self-preoccupation and egoism, and have opened themselves to the reign of God by true love of God and of their neighbor.

MEDITATION

Listen, a clear voice is calling.
It pierces the night and the darkness:

Awake and leave behind sleep and dreams—
Christ is shining in the heavens.

This is the bright time of hope.
The dawn approaches; the day begins:
A new star begins to beam,
Before whose glow the darkness flees.

From heaven is sent one as a lamb
Who will take all our sins upon himself.
In faith we turn our faces to him
And ask his forgiveness,

So that, when again he comes in light,
And his brilliance strikes the world with terror,
He may not avenge sin with punishment,
But gently gather us to himself.

Glory, honor, power and splendor
Be to God the Father and the Son,
To the Spirit, who is our protection,
Through all ages and forever. Amen.

A hymn in Lauds for Advent. Author unknown.

Third Sunday of Advent

LITURGICAL GUIDE

The third Sunday of Advent is known to many of the faithful as Gaudete (Rejoice) Sunday. The opening verse begins with this word, which, moreover, comes from the beginning of the second reading in year C: "Rejoice in the Lord always! I say it again. Rejoice! . . . The Lord himself is near" (Phil 4:4). This call to joy also finds expression in the rose-colored Mass vestments that take the place of the more somber violet and communicate a pre-Christmas joy. This distinction probably came about in imitation of the fourth Sunday of Lent, called Laetare (Rejoice) Sunday, which also has a joyful character.

In the Gospels of all three cycles the figure of John the Baptist again stands before us. From prison he sends disciples to Jesus with the question whether he is the promised Messiah. Jesus refers them to "what you hear and see," namely to those actions of the Messiah prophesied by Isaiah. He then delivers a laudatory *witness* on behalf of John and calls him the promised one who goes before the Messiah to prepare his way (A: Matt 11:2-11). John describes himself the same way (B: John 1:6-8, 19-28), while in year C (Luke 3:10-18) he gives various groups of people signs that will indicate that the Lord is near.

In all the Old Testament readings one hears joy over the blessings of the messianic kingdom. The New Testament readings retain an exhortation to patience until the coming of the Lord (A: James 5:7-10), the call to joy and the prayerful wish that the faithful may be without blemish at Christ's coming (B: 1 Thess 5:16-24), and the encouragement to joy and good conduct in light of the nearness of the Lord (C: Phil 4:4-7).

The opening prayer on this "joyful Sunday" directs our attention already to the celebration of Christmas as the feast of "love and thanksgiving." In numerous texts joy over "the gift of salvation" bursts out: Advent is the time of joyful expectation.

Spiritual Reflection

In a variety of ways the Mass for the third Sunday of Advent contains a message of joy. The words of the opening verse are taken from the second reading in year C (Phil 4:4-7). The second reading of year B likewise calls out to us: "Rejoice always!" (1 Thess 5:16). The alleluia verse before the Gospel in all three cycles indicates the source of this joy: "The Spirit of the Lord is upon me; he sent me to bring good news to the poor," a verse that is contained in the first reading of year B and continues with the words "to heal the brokenhearted, to proclaim liberty to the captives and release to the prisoners, to announce a year of favor from the Lord" (Isa 61:1-2a). The first reading from year A also speaks of great joy: "Those whom the Lord has ransomed will return and enter Zion singing, crowned with everlasting joy; they will meet with joy and gladness, sorrow and mourning will flee" (Isa 35:10).

Originally the great joy in these Old Testament readings referred to the return home from the Babylonian exile (586–538 B.C.E.). By way of comparison, a similar immense joy was experienced by West Germans in the fall of 1989 when the Berlin Wall came down, a separated part of their nation was freed from the chains of communist dictatorship, and political freedom was restored. People embraced each other on the street and tears of joy streamed down, for in freedom they could live with dignity, and life was again worth living.

The Advent liturgy therefore connects the joy of those returning from the Babylonian exile with the liberation that is bound up with the appearance of the Messiah. With his incarnation begins the great "year of the Lord's favor," freeing humanity from guilt and separation from God, the collapse of the wall that separated us; it inaugurates solidarity with the promised Messiah, who has appeared as God's loving kindness and friendship with humanity.

In the annual celebration of the approaching birth of the Savior this solidarity with Christ will not only be recalled in memory, but indeed will be newly established and secured through the presence of the Lord. Every Christian celebration is indeed not just a remembrance and memorial, somewhat like an annual birthday celebration. Rather, the celebration of Christmas becomes a faith-filled and loving encounter with the Lord of salvation and thereby a true coming of the Messiah in our own time. Thus Advent is not just a make-believe play, a pious piece of devotional theater, but a true approach of the Lord. Thus we can with complete truthfulness pray the opening prayer for the third Sunday of Advent: "may we . . . who look forward to the birthday of Christ experience the joy of salvation and celebrate that feast with love and thanksgiving."

This joyful trust also frees believers from anxious care about what still lies before us in the unknown future. In that we have been taken up into the mystery of salvation of the Lord who is present among us, we have no need to concern ourselves or become frightened. For "who will separate us from the love of Christ?" asks Paul the apostle, to whom the mystery of Christ was revealed in its depths. Distress or poverty or persecution, hunger or cold, danger or the sword? His serene response continues: "in all these things we are more than conquerors through him who loved us" (Rom 8:35, 37). Here a believing Christian gives witness in striking fashion to that glad confidence that has its foundation in a reliance on the love of Christ. "The believer already possesses his future because his future *is* Christ, and Christ is in the believer" (Karl Rahner).[2]

In the same way we should await the Lord's coming "in great power and majesty" with confidence and make our own his Advent exhortation: "when these things begin to take place, stand up and raise your heads, because your redemption is drawing near" (Luke 21:28). Those who have received within themselves the joy and trust that Advent and Christmas can bestow—people who have realized the Advent admonition to "rejoice in the Lord always"—should not miss the following exhortation of the Advent liturgy: "Let your gentleness be known to everyone" (Phil 4:5). Persons who are blessed with joy by God's love must show themselves thankful for this by the fact that their joy bursts forth as kindness to other people. Is it not said of the incarnate Son of God that he has appeared as goodness and loving kindness to humanity (cf. Titus 3:4)? Joy and kindness are siblings. "Joy seeks to communicate and share itself. It cannot simply stay at home. It leaps from person to person; it springs over borders and boundaries" (Hans Wallhof).[3]

Our joy spreads itself not only through the fact that we try to buy nice Christmas presents for the persons closest to us, but also in that we are generous to them and to everybody, every day. This graciousness inclines us to think also about those persons anywhere in the world who especially need our acts of love. It is not by chance that it is specifically during the Advent season that we are summoned especially to the charitable contribution that in Germany is called "Adveniat," thus revealing its inner connection with Advent. The Advent person who is conscious of prosperity as a gift of God will simultaneously help to prepare the way of the Lord with generosity and graciousness for those who are distant, and who will be more persuaded of the glad tidings by deeds of love than they will be by words.

MEDITATION

Listen, my heart, God has already begun to celebrate in the world and in you his Advent. He has taken the world and its time to his heart, softly and gently, so softly that we can miss it. He has even planted his own incomprehensible life in this time (we call it his eternity and we mean thereby that which is nameless, which is wholly other from the time that makes us so hopelessly sad). . . .

No brighter joy could be expected by you, poor heart, in a season of Advent that lasts for a lifetime (since *your* advent will end only when you hear the words, 'enter into the joy of your Lord'). No brighter joy, for now you still feel too keenly the harsh press of the shackles of time, even though they have already begun to fall away from your hands and feet. The only thing that must live in you is a humble, calm joy of faithful expectancy which does not imagine that the tangible things of the present time are everything. Only humble joy, like the joy of a prisoner, who will stand up even while he is still imprisoned, because, lo and behold, the bolt has already been torn off the door of his dungeon, and so freedom is already guaranteed.

Is this joy, this Advent joy so difficult? Is resignation and hidden despair really easier? . . . You have, my heart, already chosen the joy of Advent. As a force against your own uncertainty, bravely tell yourself,

'It is the Advent of the great God.' Say this with faith and love, and then both the past of your life, which has become holy, and your life's eternal, boundless future will draw together in the now of this world. For then into the heart comes the one who is himself advent, the boundless future who is already in the process of coming, the Lord himself, who has already come into the time of the flesh to redeem it.

Karl Rahner[4]

Fourth Sunday of Advent

LITURGICAL GUIDE

The fourth Sunday of Advent always falls during the second phase, when our gaze turns more strongly to the first coming of the Lord, and thus is oriented toward the celebration of Christmas. For that reason the Mass texts are chosen from passages in Scripture relating to those events that immediately precede the birth of the Lord. Thus the Gospel in year A reports Joseph's psychological distress and the clarifying embassy of the angel (Matt 1:18-24). Years B and C describe the annunciation (Luke 1:26-38) and the origin of the Magnificat during Mary's visit to Elizabeth (Luke 1:39-45).

The opening prayer ties in with the annunciation and spans the arc between the incarnation and the paschal mystery. The prayer over the gifts also mentions the mystery of the annunciation, while the concluding prayer expresses the petition: "as Christmas draws near, make us grow in faith and love to celebrate the coming of Christ our Savior."

In the Old Testament readings God gives the "sign of Immanuel" (A: Isa 7:10-14), announces that the kingdom of David will endure forever (B: 2 Sam 7:1-5, 8-12, 14, 16), and promises that the Messiah will come forth from Bethlehem and will be a shepherd to his people (C: Micah 5:1-4a).

In the New Testament reading of year A, Paul presents himself to the Roman community as the apostle called by God to proclaim the gospel of God's incarnate Son (Rom 1:1-7). The concluding doxology from the letter to the Romans constitutes the second reading in year B (Rom 16:25-27). From the letter to the Hebrews we hear in year C about Christ's prayer at his entrance into the world: "a body you have prepared for me . . . I have come to do your will, O God (Heb 10:5-10).

Thus the fourth Sunday of Advent leads us very close to the mystery of the Christmas celebration. Its statements reach a culmination in the fifth Preface of Advent in the German Missal: "For already the day of salvation blazes forth, and near is the time of our healing, for the Savior comes, our Lord Jesus Christ."

SPIRITUAL REFLECTION

The opening prayer for the first Sunday of Advent calls us to go to meet Christ on the path of righteousness and to prepare for his arrival by deeds of love. This direction could also be expressed concisely as follows: to become like the Lord in consciousness and deed. One person who succeeded in this as no other has is the mother of Jesus, who is our heavenly mother. She shines out during the dark of Advent like a glowing light, not only because of her major feast on December 8, officially entitled the feast of the Immaculate Conception of Mary, Virgin and Mother of God. In the final weeks before Christmas, the liturgy also reflects daily on her in the texts of the Mass. The Mass for the fourth Sunday of Advent alone mentions on four separate occasions the verse of Isaiah "the virgin shall be with child, and bear a son, and shall name him Immanuel [God with us]" (Isa 7:14). Thus the liturgy of this Sunday itself urges us to take Mary as the model *par excellence* for the Advent person.

So deeply and reflectively, with such profound gratitude, Mary waits as no one else does for the arrival of the Lord. She waits for nine months, like every other mother, and yet again unlike every other mother. For it was revealed to her who this child would be: "Great will be his dignity and he will be called Son of the Most High. The Lord God will give him the throne of David his father. He will rule over the house of Jacob forever and his reign will be without end" (Luke 1:32-33). Thus she awaits not only a child, but the Savior of the world, the beginning of the reign of God on earth, the salvation of all humankind. In this posture of waiting she becomes the pattern and model of the Advent person. Three characteristics mark her inner disposition:

Mary is one who reflects

The evangelists frequently mention that Mary thought deeply about the events of salvation whose witness she became, that she took them into her heart and preserved them there. Today such reflective contemplation is most often called meditation. It appears that for us modern

THE NATIVITY OF OUR LORD

General Introduction

In the understanding of early Christianity, the entire year was dominated by the central mystery that we indicate by the strange expression "paschal mystery." This refers to Christ's work of salvation culminating in his suffering, death, and resurrection. The Christian communities commemorated these events every Sunday (the weekly pasch), and in an annual feast on the Sunday after the first full moon in the spring (Easter). Apart from that there were no other Christian celebrations, with the exception of the annual memorial of specific martyrs beginning in the second half of the second century. However, from the beginning of the fourth century this situation changed. People began to unfold the content of the unique Christ-event and to act out certain parts of the event of salvation in a historical and dramatic way, staging these aspects as celebrations. Thus there developed the celebration of Good Friday as the day of Jesus' death, the memorial of the institution of the Eucharist on Holy Thursday (the beginning of the Easter triduum), and the celebration of the entrance of Christ into Jerusalem on Palm Sunday. The period after Easter showed the same tendency, as the Ascension and Pentecost became separate feasts.

The first evidence for a special Roman feast for the birth of Christ appears in the year 336. A short time later the Eastern "Christmas" of the Epiphany on January 6 was taken over, while reciprocally the Roman celebration of the birth of Christ found a home in the East. The date—and only the date—was certainly conditioned by the secular pagan feast of the birth of the unconquered sun god *(Natale Solis Invicti)*, which the emperor Aurelian introduced from Emesa in the year 274 in honor of the Syrian sun god, specifying the date as December 25.

The original content of the feast of Christmas is not only the birth of Christ, but also his conception in Mary's womb. In light of this it becomes understandable why the later feast of the Annunciation of the

Lord (which arose in the seventh century) could not establish itself as a proper feast day on March 25, a date too close to the Easter celebration.

According to a Roman tradition that can be traced back to the sixth century, every priest may celebrate three Masses on Christmas. We speak of midnight Mass *(Missa in nocte)*, the Mass at dawn *(Missa in aurora)*, and the Mass during the day *(Missa in die)*. This custom is due to an unusual characteristic of the papal liturgy about whose origin nothing more specific needs to be said here. Apart from an additional Old Testament reading added to the Christmas liturgy in the new Missal, its principal parts remain essentially the same as before. While the gospel pericope at midnight Mass proclaims the birth of Christ in Bethlehem (Luke 2:1-14), the Mass at dawn reports the encounter of the shepherds with the child in the manger (Luke 2:15-20). The Mass during the day uses the prologue to the Fourth Gospel (John 1:1-18) to proclaim the mystery of the incarnation in terms of Johannine theology.

A particular mark of reverence is conferred on the celebration of this mystery by the fact that during the Creed the congregation kneels when the verses concerning the conception and birth of Jesus are sung. Because Mary is inseparable from the celebration of this mystery, her name is explicitly mentioned in the texts inserted into Eucharistic Prayers 1, 2, and 3.

Another celebration within the Christmas liturgy is the vigil Mass or *Missa in vigilia*, which may occur before or after the first vespers of Christmas. The vigil Masses in the new rite are no longer night watches with a penitential character, but rather share in the celebratory atmosphere. The Mass on the morning of December 24 is still a Mass of Advent, with violet vestments.

In what follows we address ourselves to midnight Mass and the Mass during the day (the sung Mass).

Midnight Mass

SPIRITUAL REFLECTION

Why is it that every year at midnight Mass the church is packed to the rafters, that this is by far the most heavily attended religious service of

so will the Prince of Peace appear,
because his hour has come at last.
He unites all people, his love spreads
from mouth to mouth.
He has given us his body,
and so we celebrate the new covenant.

Huub Oosterhuis [8]

The Mass of Christmas Day

SPIRITUAL REFLECTION

The one who governs world history chose a village in Palestine to be the center of the world; the birth of a child in a stall in Bethlehem became the start of a new era. In the summer of 1969, when for the first time a human being set foot upon the moon, the president of the United States proclaimed: "This is the greatest moment in the history of the world." A Christian preacher contradicted him publicly with the words: "You are wrong, Mr. President. The greatest moment in the history of the world was the birth of the child in Bethlehem." We are reminded of this every day, whenever we write the date on a letter or a check; the numbers mean that so many years have passed since the birth of Christ.

What Christmas also means to us people of the electronic age can be illustrated by a simple simile: somewhere in a rundown castle lived an impoverished noble family. The aristocratic brilliance that once crowned it had long been lost. No one knew how they were going to survive in their complete destitution. Then one day a friend came to visit and reflected with the inhabitants on what should be done. They explored all the rooms, and at last came to the storage room. There the friend stopped before a dust-covered picture. No one had noticed it in a long time. Thick and fat streaks of oil paint, crudely drawn brush strokes suggested a cheap imitation. The friend asked if he could take this picture away to have it investigated. A restorer carefully removed the top layer of paint, then a second and a third layer that had covered the first. Finally he uncovered what was originally painted. Now the picture really began to glow, the brush strokes were more skillful, and to the connoisseur the suspicion became a certainty: this was the work of an old master, a picture of inestimable worth, for which art museums around the world would be willing to pay millions.

Do not many of our contemporaries, even when by all appearances they are doing well, nevertheless feel like poor and suffering creatures because they have lost the deeper meaning of their lives? The widely respected French philosopher Jean-Paul Sartre, one of the founders of existentialism, wrote of how the human being carries on without the slightest hope, alone and isolated, in the midst of a terrible silence without help or shelter. Round about are emptiness and nothing, and in the end death awaits. Human life, according to Sartre, is thus superfluous, absurd.

Many have applauded these words: yes, that is the way it is; Sartre puts it honestly. Have not many of our contemporaries dumped their greatest treasure in the junk room? Does not what stands written in the Christmas Gospel of the third Mass apply to many of our contemporaries: "The light shines on in darkness, a darkness that did not overcome it"? "He was in the world, and through him the world was made, yet the world did not know who he was. To his own he came, yet his own did not accept him."

What wealth the Christmas message announces: I bring you news of great joy. Today the Savior is born for you. Now your life has once again a center and goal, a hope and security. God has become a brother to us. Out of distance has come proximity, out of hostility friendship, out of poverty riches. Whoever grasps the outstretched hand of Jesus is never again alone and isolated, his or her life is not "superfluous, absurd." With Jesus as our friend and brother, we have the strength to carry forward our life. If God is for us, who can be against? All this is our great wealth, which begins with Christmas.

Nevertheless it must be admitted that in the past we Christians have allowed this precious masterpiece of our faith to be painted over with false colors, and the great feasts of our history of salvation to be so disfigured that they are barely recognizable. Christmas became the day of Santa Claus, of the decorated tree, a celebration of presents, at best a celebration of the family and of peace. Out of Easter we have created a celebration featuring the Easter egg roll and the Easter bunny; the Ascension is merged with Father's Day and Pentecost becomes an excuse for a three-day weekend or a day in the country.

Let us recognize again what a great wealth we have in our Christian faith! One of the oldest documents in Christianity, St. Paul's second letter to the Corinthians, expresses it boldly: "If anyone is in Christ, there is a new creation: everything old has passed away; see, everything has become new" (2 Cor 5:17).

MEDITATION

We shall be better able to cope with life's demands if we remain constantly aware of the directions this night provides. Let us continue our journey along the highway of life without allowing ourselves to be deterred or frightened by occasional desolate stretches. A new spirit has entered into us and we will not waver in our belief in the star of the promises or weary of acknowledging the angels' *Gloria* even if we sometimes have tears in our eyes as we join in. Many disasters have been turned into blessings because [people] have risen above them.

Alfred Delp[9]

The Holy Family of Jesus, Mary, and Joseph

LITURGICAL GUIDE

The feast of the Holy Family (Jesus, Mary, and Joseph) is celebrated on the Sunday within the octave of Christmas. However, if Christmas (and therefore also its octave day) falls on a Sunday, this feast is celebrated on December 30. This is a modern feast that has been integrated within the cluster of devotional or related celebrations and has correctly found a place in immediate proximity to Christmas.

The honoring of the Holy Family began in Canada in the nineteenth century and quickly spread to the whole world. The Holy Family was seen as a helpful model for the endangered Christian family. However, it was made universally obligatory only in 1920, initially for the Sunday after the Epiphany. The liturgical renewal of 1969 placed it on the dates mentioned above. In the liturgical texts the example of the Holy Family is put forward as a model for others.

SPIRITUAL REFLECTION

When the introductory prayer of the Mass mentions the Holy Family of Nazareth as a "shining example" for our contemporary families, does not the question naturally arise whether here we are comparing "apples and oranges," that is to say, two totally different things? Indeed, the cultural conditions and sociological pressures of those days were totally different from those of our own times. But also the personal situations of the Holy Family, such as the relationship between Mary and Joseph (sometimes referred to as a "josephite" [i. e., unconsummated] marriage), do not correspond at all to contemporary marriages and families. So what can the "shining example" be here?

Let us look for a moment at the situation of marriage and families today. Without looking at the world in a pessimistic light, it must still be admitted that, alongside many healthy families, there are unmistakable symptoms of a widespread family crisis. Who can fail to reflect on the growing number of broken marriages with all their damaging consequences for the partners and especially for the children, the rejection of the institution of marriage and family, the increasing number of couples living together "without benefit of clergy," the spreading acceptance of the decision not to have children, and, not least, the approximately 200,000 abortions that take place every year in former West Germany alone? These are in fact alarm signals of the catastrophic danger that threatens marriage and the family. Also, the statistically verifiable decrease in religious practices within the family such as attendance at Mass, grace before meals, religious instruction for children, and other Christian customs contributes to the multifaceted impression of deterioration in the contemporary family.

Is it not possible for the family from Nazareth to cast a clear beam into this dark situation? What shines out brilliantly in it is the unselfish love that fills all the members and binds them together. Here rules not heartless egoism, in which each thinks only of himself or herself, each tries to dominate the others, and there is no consideration for others, no mutual aid or forgiveness, only the slogan: I do what I want. In such a situation, the destruction of the family seems almost a foregone conclusion.

Unselfish love, which characterizes the Holy Family, pays attention to what the readings of the day say is expected of Christians: "clothe yourselves with compassion, kindness, humility, meekness, and patience. Bear with one another and, if anyone has a complaint against another, forgive each other; just as the Lord has forgiven you, so you also must forgive. Above all, clothe yourselves with love, which binds everything together in perfect harmony" (Col 3:12b-14).

But how is such an unselfish love possible? Where does one get the strength for this? The answer stands in the same reading: "Let the word of Christ, rich as it is, dwell in you" (v. 16). The word of Christ, which is simultaneously God's word, is compass and signpost for the Holy Family and for all who seek to orient themselves by their example. Mary herself acknowledges that, as the servant of God, she allows herself to be led by God's word (cf. Luke 1:38), and she expresses this basic attitude further with the words: "Do whatever he tells you" (John 2:5). When the word and will of God become the highest guide for a family, they are able to find the strength for the most difficult times, burdens, and tests, the strength to stand and remain together even during seasons that resemble the flight into Egypt, about which the Gospel of the feast tells us.

In this sense the Holy Family of Nazareth can also be in our own times a "shining example" for our endangered families. May this unselfish love, which is nourished by the Christmas generosity and good will to all people of our Savior, become at home also in our families and work its blessings. Of such families it is true, as the Second Vatican Council repeatedly emphasizes, that they are "the Church in miniature," "household churches," cells that are the building blocks of the mystical body of Christ.

MEDITATION

In the family a person can experience freedom from anxiety and loneliness, and thereby a small piece of "salvation." Here he or she is surrounded by the trust, the security, and the concern that point to our acceptance by God, and to God's fidelity.

The parents, through their relationship, create a means of access to that God who is willing to be called "Father" by us; father and mother illustrate by their lives of dedication that the true content of life does not consist in self-promotion, but rather in service to others; the children educate themselves mutually to a brotherly and sisterly love and understanding for one another.

The everyday features of family life, through their power to form us, build a path toward a faith-filled religious life: common meals, conversation, feasting and celebration, play, forms of relaxation, forgiveness freely given, family traditions. All this receives its deepening and clarification in the Mass, in the sacraments, in prayer, and preserves itself through proper conduct in the world.

German Synod (Würzburg) [10]

New Year's Day—
Solemnity of Mary, Mother of God

LITURGICAL GUIDE

The octave of Christmas concludes with the beginning of the new year. Because the pagans celebrated this day with riots and dissipation and with many superstitious practices, the ancient Church attempted to protect the faithful by offering penance services and calling for fasting. This, for example, is the tone of a sermon by St. Augustine: "Some may wish to give new year's gifts, but you by contrast should give alms. Some may wish to sing disreputable songs; you, however, should let yourselves be drawn to the word of Scripture. Some may wish to hurry to the public theater; you, however, should hurry to the church. Some may wish to get drunk; you, however, should fast" (Sermon 198:2).

The Church in Rome tried a different tack: it instituted a feast to Mary on January 1, the commemoration of her status as mother of God. During the Middle Ages this was replaced by the feast of the Circumcision and the octave of Christmas. The new liturgical calendar of 1969 returned to the original Roman custom by specifying: "January 1, the octave day of Christmas, is the solemnity of Mary, Mother of God. It also recalls the conferral of the name of Jesus."

It is properly a matter of surprise and regret that in the renewed liturgy so little attention is given to the start of the civil year. It is true that in the new Missal, in the section devoted to Masses for various public needs, the first one given is the Mass for "the beginning of the civil year," but the rubric that prefaces this Mass states curiously: "This Mass may not be celebrated on January 1, the solemnity of Mary the Mother of God." A modification of this rule would appear to be reasonable and urgent. Happily the German Missal, through a parenthetic insertion, has transferred at least the prayer of the day and the prayer over the gifts to the new year.

SPIRITUAL REFLECTION

Is it not strange? For thousands of years at the beginning of the new year many people have burst into a state of boisterous gaiety. Even in our enlightened electronic age this has not changed. Everywhere fireworks light up the sky and champagne corks pop against the ceiling. Euphoric joy marks human gatherings, only too often accompanied by alcoholic intoxication. And yet for all that not much has changed on this day, only that our spaceship earth has completed one more trip around the sun, since with its speed of approximately thirty kilometers per second it has covered a distance of 939 million kilometers. If the astronomers had not calculated this, we would hardly have noticed it.

We now stand before a new temporal unit in our lives. We wish one another happiness, health, success, and whatever else there may be. However, at the same time we realize from experience that this new year will probably not be essentially different from the old, and that in many aspects the weather forecast will be similar: alternation between highs and lows, sun and rain, storm and smog, fog and ice, accompanied by the frequent warning of the radio announcer: please drive carefully!

What do all our good wishes at the beginning of a new year depend on for their fulfillment? To this question three answers have been suggested:

Each person alone is responsible for his or her future happiness or unhappiness. Naturally this is not true for each and every detail, but we do open a way for much suffering through foolishness, selfishness, anger, a lack of self-discipline, and many other failings.

Very often we are also responsible for the happiness or unhappiness of our companions. We can make others cheerful and happy through our daily love, but can also occasion them much suffering, through thoughtlessness (e.g., a traffic accident), inconsiderateness, anger and hatred, envy and resentment.

In the final analysis, as holy Scripture tells us, the happiness of our lives depends on God's blessing, according to the verse of the psalm: "Unless the Lord builds the house, those who build it labor in vain. Unless the Lord guards the city, the guard keeps watch in vain" (Ps 127:1). At the same time we should also remain aware of the fact that God knows best what is for our own good, and that often crosses and suffering can lead to a blessing.

The liturgy of the feast of Mary the Mother of God inscribes over the door of the new year two names, as a kind of signpost and promise: Jesus and Mary. In the gospel of the day we read: "The name Jesus was given to the child." In English Jesus means "God helps." Jesus himself is the helping God, the healer of the world. However, it is not sufficient for his name to stand above the door of the new year. We must inscribe him on our hearts, on our lives; we must build him as the "way, the truth, and the life" into our everyday existence. The word of the apostle applies also to the coming year: "there is no other name under heaven given among mortals by which we must be saved" (Acts 4:12).

The gospel of the day inscribes a second name over the new year: Mary, the mother of Jesus, our heavenly mother. The opening prayer expresses our request: "May we always profit by the prayers of the Virgin Mother Mary." Mary says to us as she once said at the marriage feast at Cana: "Do whatever he tells you!" May she always remain united with us and helpful to us as our sister in faith, as an exemplar of love of God and love of neighbor, and as our loving mother.

MEDITATION

O you who hold all times in your hands,
Lord, take also the burdens of this year
and transform them into blessings.
Now that you yourself have clearly shown
in Jesus Christ the center of the ages,
lead us toward this goal.

Since all our human striving
melts before our very eyes,
bring it yourself to fruition.
The years you give to us,
when your goodness is not our guide,
go out of style like last year's clothes.

Who is here who can stand before you?
A human's day and work pass away:
You alone will endure.
God's year alone goes on and on,
every day turns back to you,
because we beat against the wind.

We expect little of our short stay.
You, however, remain who you are
for years without end.
We travel across your anger,
and yet your grace springs up
through our empty hands.

And these gifts alone, O Lord,
give substance and value to our days

that we traverse in guilt.
By them may our time be counted; that
what we have wasted, what we have ruined
may no longer appear before you.

Since you alone are eternal
and point beginning, end, and center
in the fleeting of our days,
remain graciously turned toward us
and lead us by the hand,
so that we may walk secure.

Jochen Klepper[11]

The Epiphany of the Lord
(January 6)

LITURGICAL GUIDE

The feast of the "manifestation of the Lord," named from the Greek word "Epiphany" *(epiphaneia),* is the original feast of Christ's birth in the Eastern Churches and is celebrated on January 6. Under the term "epiphany" in pagan antiquity was understood the visible appearance of a divinity or the state visit of a conqueror revered as a divinity to the towns of his kingdom.

The second half of the fourth century witnessed a mutual acceptance of the Eastern and Western feasts of the birth of Christ. From then on the East also celebrated the birth of Jesus on December 25, and united with it at the same time the arrival of the wise men from the East. They reserved January 6 for the memorial of the baptism of the Lord and the marriage feast of Cana; on that day they administered baptism.

The West, on the other hand, saw in the feast on January 6 the manifestation of the Lord before the Gentile world (arrival of the wise men), and combined the memorial of the baptism of Jesus and the marriage at Cana with the same liturgy, because on those occasions also the Savior had manifested himself in a powerful way. While at Christmas the focus is on the birth of the divine child in a stall in Bethlehem, at Epiphany it is more the greatness of this Son of God as simultaneously Messiah, king, and Savior of the world that is emphasized.

Scientists have devoted much attention to the question whether the star of Bethlehem might have been caused by a natural conjunction between the planets Jupiter and Saturn, or whether it was a miraculous luminous phenomenon that the gracious God had given the pagans as a signpost to the Christ. These, along with other questions of a historical nature, we cannot explore here.

Already quite early popular piety had turned particular attention to the wise men from the East. Indeed, they constitute the first among the Gentiles to be called and are models for all those who seek God. Over time, what had been Magi or astrologers in Matthew became kings. In the early Middle Ages they received the names Caspar, Melchior, and Balthasar. Various folk customs grew up in connection with the feast of the "three kings."

SPIRITUAL REFLECTION

The feast of the manifestation of the Lord is thoroughly illuminated by the brilliance of Christmas. Indeed, it is a Christmas feast, but still differently accented than the feast of December 25. There the newborn child in the manger stands at the center. Epiphany, on the other hand, proclaims that this poor, weak child is the Messiah and king, Lord of the entire world. His divine stature is made visible through the fact that the learned and exalted people of this earth bend the knee before him and pay him homage. The liturgy in the East and West combines with Christ's coming two events from the public life of the Lord that can also be understood as epiphanies or manifestations: the baptism of Jesus in the Jordan, when his divine origin was proclaimed, and the first miracle at the marriage feast at Cana, where by turning water into wine Jesus revealed his divine power. With Epiphany is fulfilled the prophecy of Isaiah that is the first reading of the feast:

> Rise up in splendor, Jerusalem! Your light has come,
> the glory of the Lord shines upon you.
> See, darkness covers the earth,
> and thick clouds cover the peoples;
> But upon you the Lord shines,
> and over you appears his glory.
> Nations shall walk by your light,
> and kings by your shining radiance (Isa 60:1-2).

Already in antiquity Christianity had turned its attention and veneration to these men who are described in Matthew's gospel as astrologers and who later, because of the three royal gifts, were revered as the three holy kings. Indeed, cannot and should not we also be able to discover ourselves in these three kings? Has not a star burst forth for all of us, a light appeared, a message gone forth concerning the ruler of the world born in Bethlehem? The star of faith calls all of us into proximity and community with the divine Lord. But have we really heard this call? How have we reacted to it? Have we set ourselves in motion in order to find him, the healer and Savior, to come to know him better, to enter into friendship with him? Or was the path toward him too difficult for us, our entanglement in our own concerns too great and our faith too small?

In any case, those who set out on the way, who exert themselves to become authentic Christians, do not always receive applause from their companions. Scoffers stand beside the path, and also varieties of Herods who are not happy to see someone bending the knee before a divine king—those who grasp after the means to intrigue and power, and attempt to narrow the path for believers.

As it was for the wise men from the East, our star of faith can also become dark for a while. Sometimes it is we ourselves, perhaps, who cover it, in that we push clouds before its bright light: the clouds of comfort and satiety, of poverty in our love of God and our neighbor, or perhaps also our bitterness and despair at all the troubles and sufferings that weigh us down. Periods of religious skepticism can also overtake us, times of spiritual fatigue or religious dryness. But also in such times when the star is dark, it is important that a person remain facing in the direction in which the star pointed, even if for the moment that star is not shining. Such wandering in the darkness is certainly difficult. But one day the star will shine again, clear and joyful. Then a person is happy for having stayed on the proper course.

It is said that the wise men from the East fell to the earth before the child and paid him homage. Such homage can take many forms and hues: folding the hands in prayer, bending the knee, a word of adoration, joyful praise, but also reverential silence. What is most important with each of them, however, is that the external form should have a soul, that the most intimate part of ourselves should turn lovingly toward him who is our Lord and king.

It is said of the three wise men that they brought gifts to the Christ child: gold, frankincense, and myrrh. The traditional interpretation since the days of the primitive Christian hymn composers (e.g., Caelius Sedulius, who died ca. 405) sees these gifts as symbols of christological belief, as, for example, the well-known hymn, "We Three Kings of Orient Are," makes clear:

Born a king on Bethlehem's plain, gold I bring to crown him
again . . .
Frankincense to offer have I: incense owns a deity nigh . . .
Myrrh is mine; its bitter perfume breathes a life of gathering
gloom . . .[12]

This is certainly an interpretation that is catechetically fruitful.

More recent interpretations have related these gifts to specific spiritual attitudes that the wise men (and we also!) display to the Lord as gifts, and speak of the gold of love, the frankincense of reverence, and the myrrh of our sufferings. Certainly the highest gift we can bring before the divine Lord is an interior self-surrender, as the third Eucharistic Prayer describes it: "May He make us an everlasting gift to you." This self-donation consists preeminently in this: that in what we do, and in what we do not do, we conform ourselves to the will of God.

Thus in our pilgrimage toward God, which leads us through many deserts and dark places, we can become similar to the wise men from the East in many ways; we can discover ourselves in them. "O God, may no pilgrim's way, no path toward you be too steep or hard for us."

MEDITATION

A new year has begun. During this year, too, all the paths from east to west, from morning until evening, lead on and on as far as the eye can see, through the deserts of life, with all its changes. But these paths can be turned into the blessed pilgrimage to the absolute, the journey to God. Set out, my heart, take up the journey! The star shines. You can't take much with you on the journey. And you will lose much on the way. Let it go. Gold of love, incense of yearning, myrrh of suffering—these you certainly have with you. He shall accept them. And we shall find him.

Karl Rahner[13]

The Baptism of the Lord

LITURGICAL GUIDE

When in the year 300 the Eastern Church began to celebrate January 6 as the feast of the Epiphany, besides the birth of Jesus the feast also included the arrival of the wise men from the East and the baptism of Jesus by John in the Jordan. These were tied together through the heavenly testimony to his divine sonship and the descent of the Holy Spirit, in which patristic theology saw the anointing of the Messiah and the beginning of his public ministry. At the same time the Orthodox Church converted January 6 into an important baptismal date second only to the Easter vigil.

In the Roman Church the baptism of Jesus was at first remembered in the liturgy of the hours of Epiphany. Later this memorial found its principal place on the octave day of Epiphany. The new liturgical code of 1969 placed it even closer to the feast day in that it converted the Sunday after Epiphany into the feast of the Baptism of the Lord. Where the feast of the Epiphany cannot be celebrated on January 6 it is transferred to the Sunday between January 2 and 8. If this happens to be a Sunday after January 6, the feast of the baptism of Jesus is moved to the following Monday.

At the center of what is distinctive to the celebration of the Mass stands the gospel account of Jesus' baptism, in which the three synoptic accounts are used in the corresponding three liturgical cycles. The importance of this event in the theology of salvation is powerfully communicated in the new Preface for the feast.

SPIRITUAL REFLECTION

The feast of the Baptism of the Lord concludes the Christmas season. It sweeps over the thirty years of Jesus' childhood and youth, his "hidden life," and shows us the beginning of his public ministry. This moment, which the gospels for the feast report in a few sentences, is in effect a new "epiphany." It reveals to us who Jesus is and what he intends to do.

People from Jerusalem and all over the land of Judah are hurrying to the banks of the Jordan. They have heard of John's preaching of repentance, his call to conversion. They now wish to confess their sins before him and receive the baptism of repentance in the waters of the

Jordan. One day Jesus of Nazareth is among them. He, of whom Scripture says that he has become like us in all things, with the exception of sin, he who is without sin plunges himself into the multitude of sinners. Indeed, he will take their guilt upon himself and make expiation for them. Thus in his baptism in the Jordan he expresses his solidarity with the mass of humanity bent low with sin. "Here is the Lamb of God who takes away the sin of the world," calls out John, enlightened by the Holy Spirit, as he sets eyes upon him (cf. John 1:29). Indeed, this will be the most important task Jesus accomplishes: to become the sacrificial lamb for our guilt upon the altar of the cross. As we sing and pray gratefully and trustfully in every celebration of the Mass: "Lamb of God, you take away the sins of the world: have mercy on us."

An arc connects this baptism of Jesus in the Jordan, which John performs only against his will, with that "baptism" in Jesus' suffering and death of which Luke's gospel says "I have a baptism with which to be baptized, and what stress I am under until it is completed!" (Luke 12:50). Jesus' baptism in the Jordan is also a precursor of that baptism with which at the end of his earthly path he will commission his disciples: "Baptiz[e] them in the name of the Father and of the Son and of the Holy Spirit" (Matt 28:19). Already at that time—so the Church Fathers maintain—Jesus had chosen and sanctified water as the symbol of purification for Christian baptism.

In connection with the baptism there occurs an epiphany, a revelation of Jesus' divine sonship. God's Holy Spirit hovers visibly ("like a dove") over him, and "a voice from heaven said, 'This is my Son, the Beloved, with whom I am well pleased" (Matt 3:17).

This will not remain the only testimony of his identity with God. His signs and wonders, as well as his declarations about himself, give witness to his status as the eternal Son of God. Jesus is not, as many maintain, the son of the carpenter, not just one human being among others, but also "God from God, light from light, true God from true God." As both divine and human he begins his saving work, for us and for our salvation.

The visible descent of the Holy Spirit has been understood from the very beginning as Jesus' visible consecration to the office of Messiah, as the anointing by the Spirit to the threefold office of teacher, priest, and shepherd. This is what Peter says in a homily we hear in the second reading of the Mass: "I take it you know what has been reported all over Judea about Jesus of Nazareth, beginning in Galilee with the baptism John preached: of the way God anointed him with the Holy Spirit and power. He went about doing good works and healing all who were in the grip of the devil, and God was with him" (Acts 10:37–38). Thus Jesus' baptism and the beginning of his public life become a revelation of who he is and what he is to do, of his divine-human person and his salvific ministry.

Jesus' baptism naturally turns our gaze to our own baptism and calling as well. Without presuming to exhaust the multiple statements of the New Testament and Church tradition, we can say that Christian baptism is the loving self-donation of the triune God to humankind; it is unmerited gift. It is being received into the people of God, with membership in the mystical body of Christ, an anointing by the Holy Spirit into the universal priesthood whereby all baptized persons take part in the threefold messianic charism of Christ as the supreme teacher, priest, and shepherd. However, this means that our baptism is also a calling and a mission. We are baptized not only for ourselves, but also for the benefit of others. Just as through his consecration to the ministerial priesthood a priest does not receive a gift of grace primarily for himself personally, but rather for the service of others, in the same way our own baptism is a calling to exercise our best efforts on behalf of our fellow human beings, and is thus an apostolic assignment.

Is it thus not right and proper to let ourselves be reminded by the baptism of Jesus in the Jordan of our own baptism? Through such remembrance each one of us can become aware of who we are and what we should be about.

MEDITATION

In the course of the history of salvation there are many models and signs of baptism. They show us that through "water and the Holy Spirit" God creates anew this people of the new covenant and bestows upon it the fullness of the new life that Christ possesses as the one who has been raised. Thus the Church understands the hovering of the creative Spirit over the waters at the beginning of the world, the rescue of Noah's family from the waters of the great flood, and the saving of the Israelites at the Red Sea during the Exodus from Egypt as indicators pointing toward the reality and significance of baptism.

According to the New Testament Jesus is simply the one who has been filled with the Holy Spirit. This is already "visibly" evident at the baptism in the Jordan, where God testifies that Jesus of Nazareth is God's beloved Son who will bring about the salvation of the world. After Jesus' death this Spirit is shared as a gift of the Risen One with all the members of the new people of God. Through baptism everyone who believes in Christ is integrated within the body of the Church and receives a share in the fullness of the life of Christ, in his Spirit. Thus through baptism with water and through the gift of the Spirit the people of God are continually renewed, enlivened, and at the same time empowered to testify to Jesus Christ in the world and to live according to his Spirit and his will. "We have been buried with him by baptism into death, so that, just as Christ was raised from the dead by the glory of the Father, so we too might walk in newness of life" (Rom 6:4).

German Synod (Würzburg)[14]

Source Notes, Part 1

1. Bernhard Welte in Karl Färber et al, eds. *In deiner Gegenwart. Impusel und Orientierungen für Leben aus dem Glauben* (2d ed. Freiburg, Basel, and Vienna: Herder, 1974) 52.

2. Karl Rahner, *The Great Church Year. The Best of Karl Rahner's Homilies, Sermons, and Meditations,* edited by Albert Raffelt; translation edited by Harvey Egan (New York: Crossroad, 1993) 5.

3. Hans Wallhof, "Freude, di zu uns kommen," *ferment* (Dec. 1974).

4. Rahner, *The Great Church Year*, 6–7.

5. Maria Nels, *Das Kleine Buch der Hoffnung* (Munich: ars edition, 1971).

6. Caelius Sedulius (5th c.) trans. John Ellerton (1826–1893), alt. *The Hymnal 1982* (New York: The Church Hymnal Corporation, 1985), no. 77.

7. Words from *Christian Hymnbook*, 1865, alt. *The Hymnal 1982*, no. 116.

8. Huub Oosterhuis, *Mitten unter uns* (Vienna: Herder, 1982) 67.

9. Alfred Delp, *The Prison Meditations of Father Alfred Delp,* with an Introduction by Thomas Merton (New York: Herder & Herder, 1963), "The Vigil of Christmas," 63–64.

10. Gemeinsame Synode der Bistümer in der Bundesrepublik Deutschland, *Beschlüsse der Vollversammlung* (7th ed. 1989) 1.437.

11. Jochen Klepper, "Neujahrslied," in idem, *Kyrie* (Berlin: Merseburger, 1938) 48.

12. Words and music by John Henry Hopkins, Jr. (1820–1891), *The Hymnal 1982*, no. 128.

13. Rahner, *The Great Church Year*, 106.

14. Gemeinsame Synode 1.243.

The Easter Cycle

THE PENITENTIAL SEASON BEFORE EASTER

General Introduction

HISTORICAL OVERVIEW

As early as the second century Christians prepared themselves for the celebration of Easter by a two-day fast of mourning. During the third century this was extended to include all of Holy Week, although it did not involve a complete fast. The first ecumenical council of Nicea (325) already recognizes a forty-day fasting period, the *Quadragesima*. The model for this was Jesus' forty-day fast following his baptism in the Jordan (Matt 4:2; Luke 4:1). The Church Fathers were also thinking of Israel's forty-year period of wandering in the desert, and of Moses' forty-day fast on Sinai, and the prophet Elijah on the way to Mount Horeb.

Originally the *Quadragesima* began on the sixth Sunday before Easter and extended until Maundy Thursday, the day on which, in Rome, the reacceptance of the public penitents took place. Because no fasting took place on Sundays, in the fifth century there was an effort to raise the number of actual fast days to forty. This took place in two stages: first, Good Friday and Holy Saturday were released from the Easter triduum and included within the *Quadragesima*. Later the beginning was advanced by four days, to begin with what is today called Ash Wednesday.

In the sixth century the pre-Lenten period was developed with the Sundays of Septuagesima, Sexagesima, and Quinquagesima. Here one may detect an influence of the Byzantine Church, which began the season of fasting with the eighth Sunday before Easter, because in that Church neither Saturday nor Sunday was a day of fasting.

SIGNIFICANCE

The motive for this expanded and strict season of fasting in the early Church, besides the missionary consideration in light of the significant practice of fasting among the Jews and many pagan religions, was the esteem for fasting as a means to strengthen prayer, as a way of preparing for the reception of the Spirit, as an appropriate preparation for the reception of baptism and the Eucharist during the Easter vigil by the catechumens, and as a means of enabling practical help for the poor by reducing one's personal consumption. What the Church demanded of penitents and catechumens in the way of liturgical and ascetical efforts, the faithful for the most part practiced as well in solidarity with and for one another. Solidarity with the passion of the Lord was also a powerful motive during the season of fasting.

The New Liturgical Order of *Quadragesima*

The new liturgical code omits any early period of fasting, but maintains Ash Wednesday as the beginning of Lent. Besides the term "Lent" in the Missal and the Liturgy of the Hours, the term "season of Easter penance" also appears in some areas. The thinking was that this term makes the sense of a preparation for Easter more readily apparent. It calls forth not only various acts of penance but also a greater openness to God's word and greater zeal in attending religious services and in the everyday works of charity. The Constitution on the Liturgy of the Second Vatican Council says concerning the meaning of this season:

> Lent is marked by two themes, the baptismal and the penitential. By recalling or preparing for baptism and by repentance, this season disposes the faithful, as they more diligently listen to the word of God and devote themselves to prayer, to celebrate the paschal mystery. The baptismal and penitential aspects of Lent are to be given greater prominence in both the liturgy and liturgical catechesis (*SC* 109).

As previously, the Gloria and alleluia are omitted until the Easter vigil. The Gloria, as an early Christian hymn of considerable stature, originally did not form part of the Mass liturgy. Even after its general introduction during the eleventh century it was not admitted into the *Quadragesima*. Even in the early Church the alleluia was esteemed as an ornament in the Roman celebration of the Mass because of its melodic richness. Because of its festive character it has been suppressed during Lent since the fifth or sixth century. In its place there appeared the *Tractus* as a second responsorial psalm. Today both these forms are called the "gospel acclamation."

Ash Wednesday

Liturgical Guide

With the beginning of Lent there also began a period of public penance for those who had committed an especially serious or "mortal" sin, such as denying the faith, murder, or adultery. The penitents put on a penitential garment and were sprinkled with ashes. Then, in analogy with the expulsion from paradise, came the rite of excommunication from the Church. As the institution of public penance fell away about the year 1000, the rite of a sprinkling with ashes for all believers took its place. A prayer for the blessing of ashes can be found for the first time in the eleventh century. In the following century we find the custom of making the ashes by burning the palm branches from the previous year. Pagan antiquity and the Old Testament already saw in ashes a symbol of transitoriness, sorrow, and penance. The new liturgical code retains Ash Wednesday as a day of fast and abstinence and decrees that ashes be distributed on the forehead.

According to the new Missal the blessing of the ashes takes place after the Gospel and the homily. For this purpose a choice of two prayers is provided. In both of them Easter is clearly indicated as the goal of Lent. After being sprinkled with holy water, the ashes are placed on the foreheads of the individual believers. As a verbal accompaniment, either the traditional formula "Remember you are dust and to dust you will return" (cf. Gen 3:19), or the call of Jesus at the beginning of his public ministry, "Turn away from sin and be faithful to the gospel" (Mark 1:15) can be said. The distribution of ashes may also take place as a liturgy of the word outside the context of the Mass.

The prayer over the gifts asks, "help us to resist temptation by our lenten works of charity and penance." The first two readings (Joel 2:12-18; 2 Cor 5:20–6:2) call us to penance and reconciliation. The gospel from the Sermon on the Mount (Matt 6:1-6, 16-18) warns of the corruption of good works through selfish motives. The Preface provides the classic justification for bodily fasting.

Spiritual Reflection

The loud and carefree days of Mardi Gras, or of the carnival season, are over. With Ash Wednesday another mood begins. In Mainz, a citadel of foolery, the clowns come down to the banks of the Rhine early in the morning on Ash Wednesday to wash out their empty wallets: it is also a reminiscence of happy and boisterous weeks in which many came to believe in a sort of earthly paradise, and for that purpose also dug deep into their pocketbooks.

From nearby the bells of the cathedral call out; they summon to penance. Now conversion is the order of the day; now it is proper to negotiate a new, different stretch of the annual path. Its beginning is marked in a powerful way through the symbol of ashes on the forehead: "Remember you are dust, and to dust you will return." Here human beings are called back from the realm of illusion to that of hard reality. The realization of the transitoriness of everything earthly makes us humble, drives out pride, and leads to reflection about the path and the goal of our life. The period we call Lent or the time of Easter penance shows us what is required: conversion from false ways, from incorrect modes of conduct that lead to catastrophe. Now it is appropriate to prick up our ears to receive the redemptive instruction of the gospel and of a saving faith. For that reason a second formula has also been added to accompany the rite of the distribution of ashes: "Turn away from sin and be faithful to the gospel." The smudge of ashes on the forehead with its reminder of our transitoriness is only the point of departure. It needs to be extended through conversion and belief in the one who said "I am the way, the truth, and the life."

The way Christ trod, which he calls us also to follow, does not lead into the abyss, but rather upwards: through suffering and the cross to the resurrection and glory, to a life one does not have to look back at with rage. For that reason one should not misunderstand Lent as a depressing period designed to make us sad. Rather, it will help and heal us, lift us up and strengthen us, and lead us to a joy that endures. A liturgical expression for this is found in the Preface for Ash Wednesday (Lenten Preface 4): "Through our observance of Lent you correct our faults and raise our minds to you, you help us grow in holiness, and offer us the reward of everlasting life through Jesus Christ our Lord."

With persistence and high spirits we wish to set out and stride along this new stretch of our path, the way that leads from transitoriness to a joy and glory that endures, for which Christ's resurrection is our strongest guarantee, the foundation of our hope and confidence.

MEDITATION

On the edge of the woods grows a larkspur. Its glorious blue blossom rising on its bending stalk from among the dark green curiously-shaped leaves fills the air with color. A passerby picks the flower, loses interest in it and throws it into the fire, and in a short moment all that is left of that splendid show is a thin streak of grey ash.

What the fire does in an instant, time is always doing to everything that lives . . . All this brilliant color, all this sensitive, breathing life, falls into pale, feeble, dead earth, and less than earth, into ashes. It is the same with ourselves. We look into an opened grave and shiver: a few bones, a handful of ash-grey dust.

> Remember man
> that dust thou art
> and unto dust shalt thou return.

Ashes signify man's overthrow by time. Our own swift passage, ours and not someone else's, ours, mine. When at the beginning of Lent the priest takes the burnt residue of the green branches of the last Palm Sunday and inscribes with it on my forehead the sign of the cross, it is to remind me of my death.

> *Memento homo*
> *quia pulvis es*
> *et in pulverem reverteris!*

Romano Guardini[1]

First Sunday of Lent

Liturgical Guide

The first Sunday of Lent, originally the beginning of the season of penance, receives its distinctive stamp in each of the three liturgical cycles from the Gospel about the temptation of Christ. The special Preface relates to this by emphasizing the forty-day period of fasting by the Lord in the desert, through which he "makes this a holy season of self-denial." It praises his victory over "the devil's temptations" and gives thanks that he has taught us "to rid ourselves of the hidden corruption of evil, and so to share his paschal meal in purity of heart, until we come to its fulfillment in the promised land of heaven." In this way already as we cross the original threshold, the Easter orientation of this entire period of penance is made clear.

The Old Testament readings for the first five Sundays of Lent give accounts of the most important events in the history of salvation, steering us unerringly toward the paschal mystery. The readings from the New Testament are from Paul's letters and are thematically coordinated with one of the two other readings—on most Sundays and in some cycles with both. This is especially true for cycle A, in which the Old Testament reading for the first Sunday of Lent (Gen 2:7-9; 3:1-7) tells of the temptation and sin of our first parents, and the New Testament reading (Rom 5:12-19) links Adam's sin with the "gracious gift" of Christ.

The opening verse, the opening prayer, the gospel acclamation, the prayer over the gifts, the communion verse, and the final prayer of the First Sunday of Lent are the same in all cycles. Noteworthy is the claim of the opening prayer that the *Quadragesima* is a gift of God to the community. The fruit of conversion and penance should be growth in our knowledge of Christ and our capacity to live our faith, through which the power of Christ's saving act should become visible.

SPIRITUAL REFLECTION

Even if we have already passed through the doorway of Lent on Ash Wednesday, we still expect the Mass on the first Sunday of Lent to give us direction through this time-honored period of the year, which could very well be called a spring training for the inner person, the Christian person.

The Italian author Giovanni Papini writes in his book on Christ that the history of Jesus Christ is the history of our life. In fact, it is not only Christ's words that are signposts for us. His way of life, his behavior, the events and experiences that occur in his life can also provide light and strength for Christians. We may also regard what happens to him in the desert shortly after his baptism, an account of which is given in today's gospel, as such a guiding event.

What happens there is no accident. It is expressly stated that Jesus is led out to the desert to be tempted by the devil. Jesus is preparing himself for his messianic ministry in the quiet and the deprivation of the wilderness. He does this, as did Moses and Elijah before him, through a forty-day fast. The experience of all religions and religious teachers testifies to the interior benefit of fasting. A classic expression of this could be the fourth Preface for Lent in the Missal, where it says: "Through our observance of Lent you correct our faults and raise our minds to you, you help us grow in holiness."

This fasting by Jesus is followed by the three temptations with which most of us have been acquainted since childhood. Painters from every century have interpreted them in various dramatic variations in which the artist's imagination has often been given free rein.

We do not wish to present here any scholarly reflections on whether these temptations are presented in a realistic or empirically accurate manner or whether they refer to interior, spiritual struggles, a question to which the exegetes give different answers. Both are possible, and both are compatible with our faith. In each case it is a question of an attempt by Satan to lead Jesus to make a decision that would go against his messianic mission and the will of his heavenly father. This is demonstrated with compelling brevity.

"If you are the Son of God, command these stones to turn into bread." As God's son, Jesus had the power necessary to accomplish this. However, the power to work miracles was not given to him merely for the satisfaction of his personal needs. The signs and wonders he later worked were all done with the intention of awakening and strengthening belief, not to slake his own bodily thirst or to satisfy his hunger or to give him a personal advantage. So Jesus rejects the tempter with the proverb: "Not on bread alone is man to live but on every utterance that comes from the mouth of God."

"If you are the Son of God, throw yourself down [from the pinnacle of the Temple]. Scripture has it: 'He will bid his angels take care of you; with their hands they will support you that you may never stumble on a stone.'" The goal of this second temptation is that Jesus demonstrate through a spectacular miracle before the throngs of people gathered together in the Temple square that he is the promised messianic king. On the basis of such a wondrous occurrence the throngs should lead him in triumphal procession and proclaim him king and Messiah. This is indeed the direction in which the contemporary political expectations of the Jewish people concerning the Messiah were tending. However, Jesus realizes that another route to the faith and salvation of the human race has been planned for him. He must proclaim the good news to the poor and win salvation for humankind as the suffering servant of God. Thus he again rejects Satan's suggestion and counters his quote from Scripture with another saying: "You shall not put the Lord your God to the test."

The third temptation is an enticement through worldly power with all its pomp and majesty, with an earthly paradise: "My kingdom is not from this world," as Jesus will later state before the throne of an earthly power. Rather, what he was sent to establish and intends to build up is the "kingdom of truth and life, of holiness and grace, of righteousness, love, and peace." Thus Jesus also withstands this temptation with the command: "Away with you, Satan!" and delivers himself with no ambiguity to the will of his Father in heaven.

What does this Gospel from the first Sunday of Lent have to say to someone from the first world living at the end of the second millenium after Christ? Is all this not far from our times and foreign to our own concerns? What guidance could it offer to us? I am of the opinion that even we contemporary Christians appear in it, and thus that Jesus' history is also the history of our own life, to take up Papini's suggestion. We are all called by God and God's Spirit to proceed along the way of Christ. That is the path of the divine will, the path that is illuminated by God's word and made possible by God's grace. It is a path that the Christian does not need to walk alone. He or she should be able to do it in companionship with the faithful and in union with Christ; Christ in us, we in him.

However, in walking along this path are we not also led from time to time into the desert? Are we not drawn into the desert of loneliness, where no one seems concerned about us, where we have no one to help us carry our burden when it seems too heavy for us, no one who comforts us and gives us courage and sets a good Christian example? Or do we think perhaps of the desert of physical and spiritual privation and suffering, when discouragement overwhelms us and no star appears to shine for us? When hope vanishes and our life no longer appears worth the trouble of living it, are we not in a desert of remoteness from God, of bitterness, of disappointment, yes, even of despair? And is it not the case that in such deserts voices of temptation reach our ears? "Make your life here comfortable! There is no hereafter, no life after death!" "All that is of no use." "All your efforts at proper behavior come to nothing." "Leave your ideals behind and break free of these constraints!" "Nobody cares anything about you! It's everyone for himself or herself." In these and similar tones can the voices of temptation come to us. So it is also for us contemporary Christians to arm and defend ourselves against the temptations of the evil spirits in the "deserts of our lives." Important helps to this, as Christ's words and example teach us, especially during Lent, are increased prayer, voluntary renunciation, and day-to-day concern for our fellow human beings.

MEDITATION

From time to time there occur in the lives of individual persons, as in those of entire populations, events of decisive importance. After such an event everything is different from what it was before, and there is no going back. . . . The gospels tell us in the story of the temptation of Jesus about one such event, where the whole future of humanity became open to question. . . .

If Christ as the second Adam, like the first Adam, had fallen again, an inescapable ruin would have descended upon humankind. It is helpful for us to realize that Jesus also experienced temptation and had to endure the struggle with sin.

Adolf Köberle [2]

Second Sunday of Lent

LITURGICAL GUIDE

The second Sunday of Lent is similarly shaped by its Gospel in all three cycles. It is the account of Christ's transfiguration, which is reported by all three synoptics in almost identical fashion. We will go more deeply into its significance in the following section. Here we will only notice that it appears in conjunction with the preceding prophecy of Christ's passion and resurrection as a kind of confirming manifestation of his glorification. The Preface proper to this Sunday also advances this suggestion forcefully.

The readings from the Old Testament show us an important stage in the history of salvation, in that they place Abraham, our "father in faith," at the center. The New Testament readings strengthen the community in its faith in salvation through Christ, who "has robbed death of its power" (A: 2 Tim 1:8b-10), who as risen from the dead intercedes for us (B: Rom 8:31b-34), and who as our "Savior . . . will give a new form to this lowly body of ours and remake it according to the pattern of his glorified body" (C: Phil 3:20–4:1). What is reported in the gospel concerning Christ's glory should also be entrusted to us in our passage through suffering and death.

So that even in our earthly darkness we may cling firmly to this Easter proclamation, the opening prayer asks for us: "Open our hearts to the voice of your Word and free us from the original darkness that shadows our vision." In this way the second Sunday of Lent constitutes also an intense orientation to the Easter mystery.

SPIRITUAL REFLECTION

The Gospels for the Sundays of Lent were chosen by the early Church with great care. It was a matter of giving the candidates for baptism a final instruction in the faith before their reception of the sacrament at the Easter vigil, and at the same time of leading those already baptized to a renewal of their baptism and a deepening of their faith.

If the first Sunday of Lent, from the perspective of its Gospel, can be called the Sunday of Jesus' temptation and safeguarding, today we have the Sunday of the transfiguration. What the three first evangelists report in this pericope is a magnificently composed picture of faith that is designed to encourage and embolden us in our belief. The fullness of its content can only be properly appreciated if notice is taken of the texts that precede it. For the first time Jesus has prophesied his suffering, death, and resurrection. On that account his disciples were deeply disturbed and downcast. The next saying about the necessity of denying oneself and taking up one's cross depresses them further. Perhaps they were caught up in the then widespread opinion that the Messiah would establish a triumphant political kingdom; this would have left no place for the notion of the cross and suffering for the just. Coming in the midst of their despondency, the transfiguration of Jesus confers on his words an unexpected credibility. Here the disciples experience an anticipation of the glory that Jesus will take on through the process of his suffering and death. In this way Christ's transfiguration, in conjunction with the preceding passages, is a preview of the paschal mystery.

Let us look more closely at the details of this sequence, which appears to be a superb composition by an artful master. Jesus had taken three of his apostles up a high mountain, which since the fourth century the Church Fathers have identified with Mount Tabor whose elevation of 562 meters makes possible a panoramic view of the countryside. As Jesus was praying on the ridge of the mountain, suddenly his appearance changed. "His face became as dazzling as the sun, his clothes as radiant as light" (Matt 17:2). The divinity concealed in the person of Jesus suddenly became visible. Within this radiance appeared representatives of the old covenant, Moses and Elijah, who spoke with Jesus. In Luke's gospel we read: "They . . . spoke of his passage, which he was about to fulfill in Jerusalem" (Luke 9:31). What is meant by this is that the history of salvation of the Old Testament reaches its climax in Jesus' sacrificial death and comes to completion in the paschal mystery. Is it not also clear in this scene that the reign of God in the new covenant grows naturally from the old in the same way that the trunk and crown of a tree emerge from its root system? How foolish and blind on that account appear all those who in the past, and even in the present, have believed that we should show nothing but scorn and rejection for the Old Testament!

Let us return to Mount Tabor: before the brilliance of this moment Peter cries out impulsively: "Lord, how good that we are here! With your permission I will erect three booths here . . ." (Matt 17:4). Mark and Luke add: "(He did not really know what he was saying.)" The serious topic of Jesus' sacrificial death in Jerusalem was apparently unable to penetrate his consciousness. He had only been delighted by the superficial spectacle of light. This is certainly a lesson to all believers not to become fixed on externals or side issues, but rather to penetrate to the essentials of belief.

Soon the scene changes again. Suddenly a bright cloud comes over the disciples. In the Old Testament bright clouds were always a symbol for God's special presence. From this cloud a voice comes forth: "This is my beloved Son on whom my favor rests. Listen to him." With this testimony from the heavenly Father about Jesus' divine sonship, the biblical account of Christ's transfiguration reaches its climax. This Jesus of Nazareth is God's son. Because he is, one should listen to him. To hear and obey is the appropriate and compelling response that is a logical consequence to this series of events.

This time of the transfiguration was for the disciples a period of instruction and encouragement in their belief: Jesus is both divine and human. He will walk the path of suffering and die an atoning death. Still, after Good Friday comes the resurrection. He has also prophesied this path for us, and yet for us as well are intended the words from Mount Tabor: "Do not be afraid!"

> So daily dying to the way of self,
> so daily living to your way of love,
> we walk the road, Lord Jesus, that you trod,
> knowing ourselves baptized into your death:
> so we are dead and live with you in God.[3]

MEDITATION

On the road leading to Easter, the Church does not grope its way in darkness. The faith that animates the Church is not a blind trust in God saying to it, "Go forth . . . to a land that I will show you." The luminous cloud that leads it is not only before it. The mountaintop is aglow with it. It illuminates the entire road up to its end where the Lord of glory awaits the Church. Life and immortality shine brightly through the preaching of the gospel. The glory of Christ already enfolds the believers. With the reflection of his light in their eyes, the echo of the Father's voice in their hearts, they walk toward the city that has no need for the light of the sun or of the moon; "for the glory of God [is its] light, and its lamp [is] the Lamb" (Rev 21:23).

Days of the Lord 2 [4]

Third Sunday of Lent

PRELIMINARY REMARK REGARDING
THE THIRD TO FIFTH SUNDAYS OF LENT

The Masses of the third to the fifth Sundays of Lent contain a rich variety of guidance and of the good news of salvation. This is especially true for the Gospels. They have been chosen in consideration for the candidates for baptism, but they also prove to be highly appropriate for renewing communities in their faith and love and filling them with thanksgiving for their call. In cycle A we find the pericopes about the Samaritan woman at Jacob's well (John 4:5-42), the healing of the man born blind (John 11:1-41), and the raising of Lazarus (John 11:1-45). Because of their extreme importance (Jesus gives "living water," "light," and "life"), these can also be used in cycles B and C, as the official pastoral introduction for the readings in the celebration of the Mass expressly remarks. For that reason also the present book restricts itself, as regards the third to fifth Sundays of Lent, to reflecting only on these important Gospels of cycle A, and to providing liturgical guides only for these Masses.

LITURGICAL GUIDE

As we have already remarked, the gospel about the Samaritan woman at Jacob's well has particular importance for the instruction and strengthening in faith both of the candidates for baptism and for the faithful in general. Jesus gives "living water" that bestows eternal life: a clear reference to baptism. We encounter an anticipation of this water in the Old Testament reading from the Book of Exodus, where Moses strikes water from the rock and thereby saves the people from death by thirst (Exod 17:3-7).

In the last analysis the source of living water is the love of God that is poured into our hearts through the Holy Spirit, who is given to us, as the New Testament reading announces (Rom 5:1-2, 5-6). Both the gospel acclamation and the communion verse also proclaim this "living water." The opening prayers ask God, the "Father of all goodness," to bestow on us forgiveness in our need "by prayer, fasting and works of mercy."

SPIRITUAL REFLECTION

What occurred there at Jacob's well in Samaria near the town of Shechem merits our attention. One can easily overlook significant aspects of it. The following reflection picks up only the most important parts of the extensive dialogue.

On the way from Judea to Galilee Jesus passes through Samaria. In the great heat at midday, namely at the sixth hour—at that time the hours of the day were counted from about six o'clock in the morning—he reaches the historic well of Jacob and lies down on his side, thirsty and tired. As fully human, Jesus experienced in his own body the burdens and tribulations of ordinary life, and precisely for that reason had a feeling for the afflictions of his fellow human beings.

When a Samaritan woman comes to draw water at the well, he asks her for a drink. The well is deep (thirty meters), and only with a bucket or some other vessel that could be let down with a long rope could one draw out water. The Samaritan woman shows herself surprised by this request, for between Jews and Samaritans there existed a centuries-old enmity. The two groups did not speak to one another, let alone help one another. "You are a Jew. How can you ask me, a Samaritan and a woman, for a drink?" Jesus, who sees himself in the service of all peoples, rejects such walls and hostilities that divide people and attempts dialogue between parties that are alienated.

For the woman his answer was surprising and puzzling: "If only you recognized God's gift, and who it is that is asking you for a drink, you would have asked him instead, and he would have given you living water." At that time people understood "living water" to be spring water or flowing water, in contrast to rain water collected and stagnant in a cistern. The woman reacts in a way both compassionate and mocking:

but you don't have any bucket; how do you intend to draw out living water from this deep well?

Now Jesus reveals what he meant by "living water": this well water cannot slake one's thirst indefinitely. "Whoever drinks the water I give him will never be thirsty; no, the water I give shall become a fountain within him, leaping up to provide eternal life." In the symbolic language of the New Testament, as well as in that of the psalms, "living water" means sanctification through the Holy Spirit, who leads people to eternal life; it also refers to baptism, which is sanctification through "water and the Spirit."

In the further course of the conversation Jesus answers among other things the question whether God should be worshiped on Mount Gerizim in Samaria or in the Temple in Jerusalem. Jesus teaches the Samaritan woman (and us) that what is decisive is not the place of prayer, but rather that one should pray "in Spirit and truth." "God is Spirit, and those who worship him must worship in Spirit and truth." When the woman then suggests postponing that decision until the arrival of the Messiah, Jesus wipes away all doubt: "I who speak to you am he." Not only the Samaritan woman, but also many of her compatriots thereby come to believe in him, and at their request he remains with them for two days; they confess: "this really is the Savior of the world."

Thus this dialogue at Jacob's well contains a rich revelation about Jesus: he bestows the gift of God, the "living water" that slakes the soul's thirst and fulfills the deepest longing of the human heart. He gives eternal life in that he allows himself to be baptized with water and the Holy Spirit. He is the Messiah, the Savior of the world.

In the time of the persecution of the Christians in Rome there appeared in the catacombs a wall painting in which a man is striking a rock face with a staff; from the rock a spring of water bursts forth powerfully. This man is intended primarily to represent Moses, who performed this miracle by God's power in the desert. Today's Old Testament reading reports on the dramatic circumstances in which this occurred: both people and animals were close to dying of thirst in the sweltering and waterless desert. The people's anger was directed against Moses, and it would have taken little to bring them to stone him. But God had indeed heard Moses' prayer and had not abandoned God's people. God remained true to the divine identity as YHWH, the one who says "I am here (for you)."

For the Roman Christians, Moses was a forerunner of Christ. Through his sacrificial death he made the spring of salvation burst forth from the rocky cliff of Golgotha. It flows in baptism and in all the other sacramental celebrations by which salvation is transmitted. For this deed of salvation we wish to give thanks to the "Savior of the world," especially during the holy Easter triduum for which we are preparing ourselves during Lent.

MEDITATION

Lent is springtime in the ecclesiastical year. From the planted and dying kernels of divine wheat a wonderful harvest will come, souls ripe for baptism. Lent is the ideal season to prepare for baptism.

In the ancient Church baptism was ordinarily administered to adults. After a preliminary preparation that often extended over a period of years, select catechumens were numbered among those who desired baptism and then, as postulants, given special instruction as they participated almost daily in the first part of the Mass. Furthermore, they undertook definite penitential exercises and were the object of repeated ecclesiastical exorcisms. The older Masses of Lent come from this time and frequently were designed with special reference to those preparing for baptism. This fact easily explains the confident and at times joyous tone of the Masses; the baptism motif often loses itself in the jubilant motif of Easter. Preparation for baptism had indeed a more serious side, for example, the death of the "old" man; it likewise had joyful aspects, e.g., the maternal pride of the Church, internal transfiguration, the coming Easter celebration.

For understanding the liturgy of the season this is of great importance; not the sober and serious mood of penance but a joyful anticipation of baptism is the spirit proper to the older strata of Lenten texts.

Pius Parsch [5]

Fourth Sunday of Lent

LITURGICAL GUIDE

From ancient times the fourth Sunday of Lent has borne the name *Laetare* ("rejoice") from the first word of the opening verse: "Rejoice, Jerusalem! Be glad for her, you who love her; rejoice with her, you who mourned for her, and you will find contentment at her consoling breasts." In the opening prayer and the prayer over the gifts as well, the anticipation of Easter joy rings out. The happy character of this Sunday is explained by some with the fact that we have reached the middle of Lent (from its original beginning with the first Sunday of Lent), and for that reason it is also called "mid-Lent." Others refer to the joyful rite in the catechumenate of the "opening of the ears," which takes place on the following Wednesday.

The rose-colored Mass vestments that are customary for this Sunday and displace for one day the more sober violet are first mentioned in the sixteenth century. This change of color most probably was connected with the ancient papal custom of consecrating the "golden rose" on this Sunday and bestowing it on certain worthy persons who had merited it. This custom has nothing to do with the ancient preparation for baptism; it is more closely connected with a kind of springtime celebration that was already practiced in Rome in the tenth century. In this celebration people brought freshly blooming flowers (roses?) with them to Mass and gave them as gifts to one another. From the eleventh century onward, instead of a natural flower the Pope bestowed an artificial rose crafted by a goldsmith.

The fourth Sunday of Lent in cycle A is also marked with the theme of baptism, especially through its Gospel about the cure of the man born blind. In order to understand better the connection with baptism in the story of the cure of the blind man, we must realize that the ancient Church commonly referred to baptism as "enlightenment," and to the newly baptized as "enlightened." The call and anointing of David reported in the first reading and the conferring of the Holy Spirit that follows it also count as a forerunner of baptism. The New Testament reading contains a direct reference to baptism (Eph 5:8-14): "There was a time when you were darkness, but now you are light in the Lord. Well, then, live as children of light." This passage concludes with an ancient Christian hymn about Christ and baptism. The motif of light and baptism sounds again in the gospel acclamation, in the Preface, and in the concluding prayer.

SPIRITUAL REFLECTION

We have already heard that the early Church considered the long Gospel pericopes of the third to fifth Sundays of Lent in cycle A especially suited to preparing the candidates for baptism and to deepening the faith of those already baptized, thereby leading them to a renewal of their baptismal promises. Popular opinion in Jesus' time held that every instance of bad luck or suffering was due to human guilt that was being punished by God. But where can the guilt lie for someone blind from birth who apparently could not yet have sinned? That is why his disciples asked the Lord, "was it his sin or his parents' that caused him to be born blind?"

Jesus' answer is clear: "Neither. It was no sin, either of this man or of his parents. Rather, it was to let God's works show forth in him." Jesus concludes his answer with the self-witness he has also used on another occasion: "I am the light of the world." By this he indicates that he can also extend his light to others.

Now Jesus forms a mixture of earth and saliva, applies the paste to the eyes of the blind man, and commands him to go wash himself in the nearby pool of Siloam. To everyone's amazement he comes back with his sight restored. He is led to the Pharisees. They huff and puff and twist themselves into all sorts of contortions not to have to recognize the miracle. What is not supposed to happen cannot be true. They interrogate the man born blind, then his parents, and finally the man again. They become greatly indignant and embarrassed when the cured man states: "If this man were not from God, he could never have done such a thing." Caught in a pride that blinds them, the Pharisees feel themselves cut to the quick: "You are steeped in sin from your birth, and you are giving us lectures?" And they throw him out.

What a tragedy of blindness! Presumption and arrogance prevent the Pharisees from recognizing an obvious divine sign and advancing toward belief. The seeing have become spiritually blind.

It is otherwise with the man born blind. Jesus meets him shortly afterward and asks him, "Do you believe in the Son of Man?" He answers, "Who is he, sir, that I may believe in him?" When Jesus allows himself to be recognized as such, the healed man falls down before him and confesses, "I do believe, Lord." Thus the blind man learns to see in a double sense: he sees with the sight of the eyes and also with the light of faith. They both came as a gift to him from the one who is "the light of the world."

Does not this gospel also hold up a mirror to modern people that can assist them toward self-recognition? In a play written by Carl Zuckmayer in 1946 entitled "The Devil's General," a young lieutenant asks the general, "do you believe in God?" The general at first gives an evasive response: "I have never met him." He follows this with the telling admission: "however, that was my fault. I did not want to encounter him, for I feared what consequences there might be for my life."

With regard to the incarnate Son of God, are we not all placed in the same position and before the same decision: either to believe in him and to draw the consequences for our life or to avoid him entirely and thus to decline belief? However, the person who refuses belief in many ways resembles the Pharisees who do not believe: they have eyes but they do not see; in fact, they do not wish to see!

However, anyone who decides to believe must take to heart the first two verses of today's New Testament reading: "There was a time when you were darkness, but now you are light in the Lord. Well, then, live as children of light." A life lived in the light of Christ is for many people the only Bible they still read, and is more persuasive than many words.

MEDITATION

Through the sending of the eternal Word into our world, the one who is both divine and human became the "true light, which enlightens everyone" (John 1:9). In the old covenant the Word appears in veiled fashion under the name of "wisdom": it is "a reflection of eternal light" (Wis 7:26). The prophets proclaim the "great light" (Isa 9:2; cf. 60:19-20) for which humanity, which sits "in darkness and in the shadow of death" (Luke 1:79), yearns. When the Savior arrived, the ancient Simeon welcomed him as the "light for revelation to the Gentiles" (Luke 2:32), and Christ testifies to himself this way when he cries out: "I am the light of the world. Whoever follows me will never walk in darkness but will have the light of life" (John 8:12; cf. 9:5). This light is poured out at baptism into the souls of the catechumens. That is why in the early Church this sacrament was called "enlightenment" (*illuminatio, photismos;* cf. Justin Martyr, *Apology* 1).

"There was a time when you were darkness," writes St. Paul to the Ephesians (Eph 5:8), "but now you are light in the Lord. Well, then, live as children of the light." Countless New Testament passages echo this theme. "Light is the element in which the life of the Christian takes place and comes to its fullness" (Johannes Pinsk). About this completion, as it will be experienced for eternity through Christ, the book of Revelation (21:23) gives a suggestion: The heavenly city needs neither sun nor moon, for it will be illuminated by the glory of God. That is why we speak of the light of glory with reference to fulfillment in eternity and pray for those who have died that "eternal light may shine upon them."

No less numerous than the scripture passages are the liturgical texts that speak of the divine light, welcome and cherish it in hymns, or make use of its symbolism during the blessing of candles (e.g., at Candlemas and the Easter vigil).

Dorothea Forstner[6]

Fifth Sunday of Lent

LITURGICAL GUIDE

Before the new liturgical order of 1969 the fifth Sunday of Lent introduced "Passiontide," so called because the sufferings of Christ received more emphasis. The Sunday itself was called Passion Sunday, but also *Iudica* after the first word of the Latin introit. The suppression of this designation in the official commentary on the foundations of the liturgical year is justified by the intention "to preserve the unity of Lent" (*GRC* I.I.2.B.1). As a matter of fact the entire Lenten period is equally pervaded by the paschal *transitus* of the Lord.

Beginning in the twelfth or thirteenth century it was also customary to cover all crosses and pictures in the church starting with this Sunday.[7] The Roman Missal of 1970 states that this custom may be retained if the local bishops' conference considers it appropriate. The German Missal of 1975 retains the custom.

The fifth Sunday of Lent in year A derives its particular accent from its gospel about the raising of Lazarus (John 11:1-45). Jesus announces and shows himself to be "the resurrection and the life" (v. 25). The two preceding readings also speak of the life-giving Spirit of God (Ezek 37:12b-14; Rom 8:8-11). Thus the liturgy of the word in the celebration of this Mass leads us into the center of the Christian message of salvation in that it proclaims that death is overcome. The Preface for this Sunday does this with the words: "As a man like us, Jesus wept for Lazarus his friend. As the eternal God, he raised Lazarus from the dead. In his love for us all, Christ gives us the sacraments to lift us up to everlasting life."

The verses intoned between the readings are also filled with this confidence: the responsorial psalm speaks of trust in God's word and the forgiveness of sins, while the gospel acclamation seizes upon the central sentence of the gospel (v. 25). The opening and concluding prayers ask that we remain as living members in the love and the body of Christ.

SPIRITUAL REFLECTION

No other suffering stirs people so deeply and sorrowfully to the core of their being as does the death of a loved one. At all times, among all peoples and cultures, death ranks as the greatest evil, the most severe danger threatening human happiness. Where it strikes, lamentation and wailing reign. The sorrow and tears fill not only hours and days, but often months and years.

The Gospel for the fifth Sunday of Lent, from the eleventh chapter of John, reports on the occasion of a death in a family strongly linked to Jesus by friendship. Lazarus of Bethany, a village near Jerusalem, brother of the sisters Martha and Mary frequently mentioned by the evangelist, is severely ill. When Jesus hears the news, he says: "This sickness is not to end in death; rather it is for God's glory, that through it the Son of God may be glorified."

Shortly before this, at the feast of the consecration of the Temple in Jerusalem, Jesus had become involved in a heated argument with some other Jews. They are now seeking to arrest him because of his supposed blasphemy. He eludes their grasp and finds himself, when the news reaches him, east of the Jordan. For a while he delays his return, and when he enters Bethany, Lazarus has already been in the grave for four days.

Many Jews from the district around Jerusalem have assembled in Lazarus's house to mourn him. Martha hears that Jesus is approaching Bethany and hurries to meet him. Not without a slight reproach about his late arrival does she say, "Lord, if you had been here, my brother would never have died. Even now, I am sure that God will give you whatever you ask of him." Jesus answers her: "Your brother will rise again." When Martha interprets these words as referring to the resurrection on the last day, Jesus utters a truly revolutionary message. He promises nothing less than the destruction of death: "I am the resurrection and the life: whoever believes in me, though he should die, will come to life, and whoever is alive and believes in me will never die." Jesus realizes that with these words he is proclaiming something utterly unbelievable. Thus he asks Martha, "do you believe this?" She summons all her powers of faith and says, "yes, Lord, I have come to believe that you are the Messiah, the Son of God: he who is to come into the world."

There then follows a moving encounter when Martha's sister Mary meets Jesus. "When Jesus saw her weeping, and the Jewish folk who had accompanied her also weeping, he was troubled in spirit, moved by the deepest emotions." On the way to the grave Jesus could not keep back his tears. Jesus wept. We see that Jesus is not only God, he is also human, with a heart that feels all human emotions, with a heart that is compassionate with human suffering, a man who feels himself one with suffering humanity.

Jesus now commands the doors of the stone grave to be taken away and says with a loud and commanding voice, "Lazarus, come out!"

Now follows something incomprehensible. The dead man, about whom Martha shortly before had said, "Lord, it has been four days now; surely there will be a stench," now emerges as a living person among the living. Jesus has followed his words about the resurrection with a deed, just as on another occasion he calls out "even though you do not believe me, believe the works." As a matter of fact, many of the Jews who were present did come to believe in him at this hour. However, the Pharisees who heard about this new sign from the hated Nazarene decided that day to kill him (cf. John 11:46-53).

What this Gospel reports is of great importance for us from numerous perspectives: it strengthens our belief in Jesus' divine sonship. He is the promised Messiah, the Savior of the world. For that reason everything that he says is divine revelation and a sound guide for all times and all peoples. Jesus demonstrates by raising the dead, and not least through his own resurrection, the truth of his mission: "I am the resurrection and the life: whoever believes in me, though he should die, will come to life, and whoever is alive and believes in me will never die." Already at this point he is planting the seed of immortality in us. Thereby he has removed the most painful thorn—its hopelessness—from earthly death. "The sadness of death gives way to the bright promise of immortality. Lord, for your faithful people life is changed, not ended. When the body of our earthly dwelling lies in death we gain an everlasting dwelling place in heaven" (Preface of Christian Death 1).

For that reason we should not mourn like those who have no hope. Even if at the death of specially loved persons we are not spared sorrow and tears, we still know that our fate is not eternal separation, but eternal community in God. "What we bury in the coffin is the robe of earth. What we love remains for eternity."

MEDITATION

We are not made for death.
Our God is a God of the living.
He does not abandon his Son in the abode of the dead.
He does not suffer his holy ones to decay.
Over every Christian grave glows the Easter sun
of hope: we will rise again.
Christ is the firstborn,
the first one risen from the dead.
I am the resurrection, he said;

the hour is coming, and now it is here,
in which the dead hear the voice of God's Son.
I am life. Whoever believes in me will live,
even if they die. And anyone who lives and believes in me
will never die. . . .
In baptism we were drawn with him into death
and were buried with him.
But if his death is also our death,
then his resurrection will also be our own . . .
The path that leads from death to life has been opened up.
At the moment of death, life is born.
Christ has overcome death.
Death's coils are destroyed, its chains broken.
Death's power to hold its victim is no more.
Death itself has died; life lives.

Walter Risi [8]

Palm Sunday

LITURGICAL GUIDE

With Palm Sunday begins "Holy Week," in German called *Karwoche* (from *kara* = lamentation, mourning), which concludes with the high point of the Church year, the Easter triduum. Among the six Sundays of Lent, Palm Sunday occupies a preeminent position. The official name for this Sunday, "Palm Sunday of Christ's Passion," makes clear that two aspects come together in today's liturgy: the memorial of Jesus' entrance into Jerusalem when the throngs welcomed him with joyous acclaim, and the memorial of his passion.

Concerning the procession with palms, which was held in Jerusalem as early as the year 400 and for which the new liturgical code provides three possible forms, we will only remark here that it is not intended as a kind of historical imitation or mystery play, but rather as a public proclamation of discipleship in faith and grateful love.

In the celebration of the Mass according to forms 1 and 2 all the introductory rites, with the exception of the opening prayer, are omitted when Mass is preceded by the palm procession. In form 3, or if there is no preceding procession, the opening verse expresses joy at Jesus' messianic entrance into Jerusalem. The Mass celebration is completely shaped by the theme of Christ's redemptive suffering. This is especially true of the Gospel, which consists of an account of the passion according to Matthew, Mark, or Luke, according to the cycle for that year.

The Old Testament reading, from the third "Servant Song" (Isa 50:4-7), leads into the responsorial psalm (Psalm 22), which has the response: "My God, my God, why have you abandoned me?" The New Testament reading (Phil 2:6-11) shows how Jesus' obedience unto death, "even death on a cross," is followed immediately by his exaltation. Verses 8 and 9 return also in the gospel acclamation, and are repeated on Good Friday. The Preface describes Christ's paschal mystery concisely and with lapidary brevity, and with an almost Easter joy. The opening and concluding prayers both refer to Christ's central, saving act, while in the prayer over the gifts we ask for reconciliation through Christ's sacrifice.

Spiritual Reflection

Palm Sunday begins the most important, holiest week in the entire Church year. It is not only the week of sorrow and lamentation, but also the week of those events of salvation we call the paschal mystery. The word "paschal" comes from the Hebrew *pesach* and means transition or passage; it refers to the essential saving deed of Christ. The central phrases of a classic scriptural text that is also used at the Mass on Palm Sunday read: "he humbled himself, obediently accepting even death, death on a cross! Because of this, God highly exalted him and bestowed on him the name above every other name" (Phil 2:8-9). Here in the idiom of an ancient hymn the paschal mystery is sung as the passage of the one who is both divine and human through suffering and death to resurrection and glory. We stand here before an indestructible act of divine salvation, which in love for us God has initiated and carried out through Jesus. We celebrate this divine act of salvation in the week that runs from Palm Sunday to Easter.

We should notice something fundamental about this celebration: it is not only a memorial of something in the past. Rather, behind the concealing veil of the sacramental signs this salvific work of Christ becomes a real and effective presence. Especially in the celebration of the Eucharist, the exalted Christ becomes present with his willing self-abandonment, his obedience under suffering, and his intercession for all humankind. He becomes present as the high priest of the new covenant with his body that has been transfigured and sacrificed for us, with his blood that has been poured out for us, hidden behind the eucharistic signs of bread and wine.

Among the people who met Jesus that day with palm and olive branches and accompanied him toward Jerusalem were, as John's gospel tells us, especially those people who had witnessed, by sight or report, the raising of Lazarus, had become believers, and now gave testimony on his behalf (John 12:17). The cries of "Hosanna"—which means "come to our aid"—are shouts of homage to the Lord of life and death; they are cries of yearning for the coming of the messianic reign.

Here in Jerusalem will now be fulfilled what in the same place on the fortieth day after Jesus' birth the aged Simeon prophesied: that he would become a sign of contradiction and the occasion for the fall and rise of many (Luke 2:34). In the first days of this week this develops into an increasingly intense conflict with the Pharisees and scribes until, after the Last Supper, he is arrested, subjected to degrading torture, and put to death on the cross. This is the subject of the passion texts on Palm Sunday and Good Friday.

That is the reason why the services on Holy Thursday evening and on Good Friday have particular power and relevance. The liturgical highpoint, however, will take place at the Easter vigil when the Easter candle is lit, the Gloria and alleluia ring out again after an interruption of many weeks, and our joy over the presence of the resurrected Lord finds manifold expression. As many people as possible should attend these services, joining themselves in faith and love with the crucified and risen Lord who awaits each one of us in love.

MEDITATION

It is rare for a liturgical festival to offer us as intensive an interpretation of our own life and destiny as does Palm Sunday. Still more: if we do not remain spectators but become participants we experience the redemption of our own life and destiny through the life and destiny of Christ, in that his way becomes our own and our way becomes his; his fate becomes our own and our fate becomes his; everything we humans do and suffer becomes immersed in the actions and sufferings of God's Son.

In his death on the cross Christ, the Son of God, completed his incarnation, for death and dying is, if not *the,* still *an* essential basic experience of humanity. In the liturgy this entire trajectory is described:

its starting condition, its course, its goal. Being human means being poor and brings suffering with it. All life is suffering. Why do we have to suffer because of one another? Why must the heart that would pour itself out be a heart that is pierced? Why must the one whose "food it was to do the will of the Father" bleed to death on the cross and cry out to this same Father: "My God, my God, why have you abandoned me?" in order to enter into his glory?

We do not know the answer. It would be presumptuous to want to say more than the one who died with this "why?" upon his lips. We know only that it is indeed so, and that this is the unique path to our salvation.

Bernardin Schellenberger[9]

Source Notes, Part 2

1. Romano Guardini, *Sacred Signs,* translated by Grace Branham (St. Louis: Pio Decimo Press, 1956), "Ashes," 53–54.

2. Adolf Köberle, *Die Stunde der Versuchung* (Hamburg: Furche-Verlag, 1958) 69.

3. "Eternal Lord of Love," stanza 2. Words by Thomas H. Cain (b. 1931). *The Hymnal 1982,* no. 149.

4. Robert Gantoy and Romain Swaeles, eds., *Days of the Lord* 2. English translation of *Jours du Seigneur* (Brepols: Publications de Saint-André, 1988) by Madeleine Beaumont (Collegeville: The Liturgical Press, 1993) 80.

5. Pius Parsch, *The Church's Year of Grace* (2nd ed. Collegeville: The Liturgical Press, 1964) 2:69.

6. Dorothea Forstner, O.S.B., *Die Welt der Symbole* (Innsbruck: Tyrolia, 1961) 96.

7. For more on this, see Adolf Adam, *Das Kirchenjahr mitfeiern,* 5th ed. (Freiburg: Herder, 1989) 94–95.

8. *Gotteslob. Katholisches Gebet– und Gesangbuch* (Stuttgart: Katholische Bibelanstalt, 1975) 791, 2.

9. Bernardin Schellenberger, *Nacht leuchtet wie der Tag. Glaubenserfahrungen* (Freiburg, Basel, and Vienna: Herder, 1981) 82–84, 87–88.

THE EASTER TRIDUUM

General Introduction

The early Church celebrated the entire paschal feast in its fullness during the single Easter night until morning on Easter day. Only from the beginning of the fourth century, with the coming of a more narrative and imitative form of representation, was this content spread out and its various aspects more sharply distinguished. In this way there developed "the most holy triduum of the crucified, buried, and resurrected Lord" (St. Augustine). The General Norms for the Liturgical Year state: "The Easter triduum of the passion and resurrection of Christ is thus the culmination of the entire liturgical year" (18). It "begins with the evening Mass of the Lord's Supper, reaches its high point in the Easter vigil, and closes with evening prayer on Easter Sunday" (19).

The history of the triduum celebration had left it very much in need of reform. Under Pope Pius XII there appeared, in 1951 and 1955, two reforming decrees that were a valuable anticipation of the postconciliar liturgy of the new Roman Missal of 1970. What follows is based on the revised form of the Missal of 1973.

There are two reasons why this triduum should begin with the evening of Holy Thursday: on the one hand it accords with the ancient Jewish convention that a day begins with the previous evening, so that the celebrations of Sundays and feastdays begin liturgically with evening prayer on the previous day. The second reason is that in Jesus' last supper his sacrificial death on the cross is sacramentally anticipated, and the washing of feet on this evening is a clear sign of his self-giving love. Besides that, Jesus' agonized prayer on the Mount of Olives, the betrayal by Judas, and Jesus' arrest on that evening constitute the start of his passion.

Holy Thursday

LITURGICAL GUIDE

The German name for this day *(Gründonnerstag)* derives from a Middle High German verb that persists to this day in the words *grienen* and *greinen*. It must be related to the fact that earlier it was on this day that those faithful sentenced to an ecclesiastical penance, also called the "mourners," were allowed to rejoin the Church community. Their release from penitent status also led to the term "Day of Release." On occasion we also come across the term High Thursday.

The liturgy of Holy Thursday evening is shaped by the memorial of Jesus' last supper and the institution of the Eucharist. Significant is also the rite of foot washing that accompanies it as the symbol of a love that expresses itself as service. Apart from the episcopal "chrism Mass" in the morning, normally only the Mass of the Lord's Supper may be celebrated on this day. The entire community should take part in this service.

The opening verse already proclaims and praises the paschal mystery of the Lord (Gal 5:14) through which we are "saved and made free." "During the singing of the Gloria, the church bells are rung and then remain silent until the Easter Vigil, unless the conference of bishops or the Ordinary decrees otherwise" *(Sacramentary)*. According to ancient custom, the same holds true for the organ, even though the Missal contains nothing about it. The silencing of this festive and boisterous instrument was interpreted as a "fasting for the ears," similar to the "fasting for the eyes" achieved by covering the statues and crucifixes.

The opening prayer focuses on the institution of the Eucharist as sacrifice and banquet of love. The Old Testament reading (Exod 12:1-8, 11-14) recounts the slaughtering and eating of the paschal lamb in Egypt; the lamb's blood on the doorposts and lintels of the houses became a saving sign for Israel. The responsorial psalm (Psalm 116) gives thanks for this saving act of God in history and directs our thanks through its verse response to the "cup of salvation" (cf. 1 Cor 10:16). The New Testament reading (1 Cor 11:23-26) gives an account of the institution of the Eucharist. The gospel acclamation links this with the Gospel, proclaiming the new commandment "love one another as I have loved you." The Gospel pericope, John 13:1-15, reveals Christ's deepest orientation, which becomes visible in the washing of the feet of his disciples: not domination, but service.

Before the reform of 1955 the washing of the feet as the symbol of a love that serves was prescribed only for episcopal and monastic services. However, the new code offers it to all church communities, "depending on pastoral circumstances." For the period during the preparation of the gifts, the Missal prescribes the verse "the love of Christ has gathered us together into one," in praise of a love that serves. The prayer over the gifts is a reminder that in this hour also the work of salvation comes to its completion in us. The Preface praises the institution of the eucharistic celebration (Preface of the Holy Eucharist 1). For Eucharistic Prayers 1-3 special insertions are provided.

After the concluding prayer the hosts that have been consecrated in advance for Good Friday are brought to the tabernacle in a nearby chapel, where a nocturnal vigil may take place. The altar is then stripped.

SPIRITUAL REFLECTION

What happened in Jesus' life on the evening of Holy Thursday is like an open book. Here one can read the deepest motivations in the life and death of Jesus, and thus what the guidelines should be in the life of any Christian. What transpired on the evening of Holy Thursday and is expressed in the Mass of the Lord's Supper is like an advanced course in Christian faith and Christian life. I will choose three important events of this evening:

Jesus institutes the sacrament of his suffering and death.

Following Jewish custom and law Jesus celebrated the so-called paschal meal on the first day of unleavened bread, the Jewish Passover. This is an annual reminder of the liberation of Israel from slavery in Egypt. The gospel of John introduces this meal scene with the striking remark: "Jesus realized that the hour had come for him to pass from this world to the Father. He had loved his own in this world, and would show his love for them to the end."

Within the context of this meal he inaugurates the sacramental memorial of his suffering and death by giving bread to his disciples and saying, "This is my body to be given for you. Do this as a remembrance of me" (Luke 22:19). "In the same way, after the supper, he took the cup, saying, 'This cup is the new covenant in my blood. Do this, whenever you drink of it, in remembrance of me.'" Paul continues, "Every time, then, you eat this bread and drink this cup, you proclaim the death of the Lord until he comes!" (1 Cor 11:25-26). It was Jesus' wish that his sacrificial, life-redeeming deed should remain always with us, not only as a memorial but rather as an effective and salvific presence. Christ is active among us as the one who offers himself to the Father for our sake and pours out his blood for us.

Jesus illustrates his serving and sacrificial love symbolically through the washing of the feet.

At the time of Jesus it was the task of servants and slaves to wash the dust of the highway from the feet of their master and his guests. By washing the feet of his own disciples, Jesus now breaks through the conventional arrangement of lordship and service. Already on an earlier occasion Jesus had given his disciples the admonition, "whoever wishes to be great among you must be your servant, and whoever wishes to be first among you must be your slave; just as the Son of Man came not to be served, but to serve, and to give his life a ransom for many" (Matt 20:26-28). Jesus now follows up his words with a clear example, and he concludes with the pointed admonition: "What I just did was to give you an example: as I have done, so you must do" (John 13:15).

In the hour of his agony at the prospect of death, Jesus turns himself toward the will of the Father.

After Jesus had concluded the last supper with the appropriate hymns of praise, he went with his disciples to the Mount of Olives. There "he began to experience sorrow and distress. Then he said to them, 'My heart is nearly broken with sorrow.' . . . He . . . fell prostrate in prayer. 'My Father, if it is possible, let this cup pass me by. Still, let it be as you would have it, not as I'" (Matt 26:38-39). He thus consciously handed himself over, for all the terrible things that would happen in the hours to come, entirely to the will of his heavenly Father. What earlier he had described in words to his disciples as his fundamental orientation: "My food is to do the will of him who sent me and to complete his work" (John 4:34), he now demonstrates graphically on the Mount of Olives.

In this sense the events of Holy Thursday are indeed like an open book, an advanced course in Christian faith and wisdom. In Jesus' words and deeds we can read that obedience to the will of God and a serving love for our fellow human beings are the deepest guidelines in Jesus' life, and for that reason must also be such in our lives. In this hour of the Mass of the Lord's Supper we wish to make ourselves cognizant of the fact that

> The same Christ who held his last supper with his disciples is in our midst.
>
> The same Christ also extends to us his body offered for us and his blood poured out for us.

The same Christ desires to include us in his offering to the Father, in view of which we say in the third Eucharistic Prayer, "May he make us an everlasting gift to you."

Moreover, those who allow themselves to be swept up in this loving and self-sacrificing offering to the heavenly Father will receive the strength to shape their own lives according to God's will, to carry their daily cross without falling, to grow in a love that serves their fellow human beings, and to experience therein the fullness of meaning of their own lives.

MEDITATION

The love of Christ encircles us all like a ring.
Let us praise him with shouts of rejoicing!
Let us draw near to the living God with trepidation
and carry one another's burdens with a good heart.

Those who cultivate no love live in darkness;
They live only for themselves, and decay into death.
Hence let us love one another without deceit,
and on the bright path keep our spirits awake . . .

As love finds unity even among those who are far apart,
discord divides even those who have been joined.
Let the minds of brothers and sisters be undivided and one;
Love alone must direct our actions.

Since we have now been united in one love,
let us take care that no hate disturb this unity!
May strife, discord, and angry spirits be far from us,
and may Christ the Savior dwell in our midst!

"Where people have come together," says the Lord,
"to call out my name of one accord,
even if it be two or three brothers and sisters together,
I am there among them with my fidelity."

True love never grows cold: it lasts forever.
Growing steadily it unfolds in two directions:
To love God and human beings at once and together,
this is the command of Jesus Christ, our brother.

Paths steep and narrow lead us upwards;
Highways wide and easy invite us downwards.
Discontent brings eternal strife to all sinners,
But compassionate love gives life.

With our whole heart let us love the Lord God,
whose love is to be preferred to all others.
And on God's account let us also love our neighbors,
even those who have injured us, as we love ourselves.

Let us direct our prayers to the Most High:
May God graciously bestow peace upon our days,
drive away envy and division, disputes and discontent;
May faith, hope, and love abide in us all.

Hymn Congregavit *(Paulinus of Aquileia, ca. 800)*

Good Friday

LITURGICAL GUIDE

Good Friday, as the day of Christ's death (Fourteenth Nisan in the Jewish calendar, which that year was a Friday), has always been observed as a day of sorrow and sympathetic fasting. This sorrowful fasting became so rooted in the consciousness of the early Church that in the West it was at times extended to all Fridays and Saturdays of the year. Today the Church still maintains Good Friday as a day of fasting and complete abstinence from meat.

The new order for the Good Friday liturgy of 1955 (introduced by Pius XII) was taken over in its essentials in the postconciliar Missal of 1970. This is also true for the time of the celebration (three P.M. as the hour of Christ's death), although for serious pastoral reasons a later hour may be chosen. In place of the black Mass vestments, red is worn—the color of the martyrs, who have their model and precursor in Christ and in whose obedience unto death their own sacrifice and triumph has its foundation.

The Good Friday liturgy consists in the liturgy of the word, the veneration of the cross, and the distribution of communion. At the beginning, after the priest's prostration before the bare altar and a prayer from the celebrant's chair, there is a reading from the Old Testament (Isa 52:13–53:12, the fourth Servant Song) with Psalm 31 as the responsorial psalm, then the New Testament reading (Heb 4:14-16; 5:7-9) with the gospel acclamation (Phil 2:8b-9), the passion account of John and, where possible, a short homily. The following "general intercessions" are in ten sequential groupings that refer to the Church, the faithful, the government, and all of suffering humanity.

There are two forms for the veneration of the cross. In the first (traditional) form the cross is uncovered in three phases, after which each time "this is the wood of the cross . . ." is intoned with the community responding. The uncovered cross is installed where it can be viewed by the entire congregation and venerated by the clergy and faithful with a genuflection, bow, or kiss. In the second form the priest (with his assistants) takes the uncovered cross to the church entrance and carries it toward the sanctuary, pausing three times and intoning "this is the wood of the cross . . ." All the rest follows the first form. During the veneration of the cross the time-honored hymns for the veneration of the cross are sung either by a choir or by the community.

For the celebration of communion the hosts consecrated in advance on Holy Thursday are brought to the altar from the place where they have been reserved. After an Our Father and the embolism, the priest lifts the host and says the customary "This is the Lamb of God . . ." and receives the Lord's body. The faithful then receive communion. After a period of silent prayer the priest says the concluding prayer and the final blessing.

SPIRITUAL REFLECTION

Place a blind person before a painting, explain to him or her its extraordinary composition, the magnificence of its colors—to the blind person this all remains closed, for he or she lacks eyes that can see. Is it not somewhat similar with us when the Church in this hour of Jesus' death places us before the powerful depiction of Christ's suffering and death? In order to comprehend all of its dimensions to any degree we require that inner spiritual power that one could call the eyes of faith. It is with these that we need to look at the mystery of Good Friday, as the readings, prayers, and liturgical rites present it to us.

Holy Scripture leaves no doubt that Jesus' suffering and death were a voluntary expiation for humanity's guilt due to sin. "Behold the Lamb of God, who takes away the sins of the world," as we say in the words of John the Baptist in each celebration of the Mass. The prophetic gaze of Isaiah the prophet already reveals it to us in today's reading: "it was our infirmities that he bore, our sufferings that he endured, while we thought of him as stricken, as one smitten by God and afflicted. But he was pierced for our offenses, crushed for our sins; upon him was the chastisement that makes us whole, by his stripes we were healed."

This atoning sacrificial death of Christ teaches us a threefold lesson:

Christ's death shows us *the extent and gravity of humanity's guilt due to sin.*

Atonement means the reparation of wrong and indebtedness. If Christ has now achieved so great an expiation, how can one then minimize human sinfulness? Large segments of our society have simply stricken sin from their consciousness; they can muster only a sympathetic smile for those who still take sin seriously. However, Christ's cross speaks another language. In mortal sin humanity tears itself loose from the divine order, from the divine will, and as for obedience, announces: "I am my own master; I can do what I like. Not your will, but mine be done!" This was the cry of Lucifer that humanity may adopt, a revolt of creation against its creator and Lord.

Christ's expiating sacrificial death reveals *the magnitude of divine love.*

Anyone who sacrifices his or her own life out of love for fellow human beings has certainly demonstrated love. Memorials have quite appropriately been set up to honor such individuals. The unique extent of God's love consists, however, in the fact that God's Son sacrificed himself, died for us, when we were still sinners (cf. Rom 5:8). Thus the cross on Golgotha proclaims to us that God's love for us knows no limits. Jesus' arms stretched wide on the cross are like the symbol of this love with which he wants to embrace us all (cf. John 12:32). Because this symbol radiates security and confidence, our ancestors did not want it to leave their sight; they placed it not only in their churches and homes, but also along their paths to the fields, in groves of trees, and on mountaintops. In one forest shrine I found this striking inscription:

> Why this cross that here stands by the path?
> It will to the traveler who passes by this way
> a good word of consolation say:
> The Lord has borne your guilt.

Christ's atoning sacrificial death speaks to us of *the richness of our salvation.*

If Christ has paid such a great price, if he has made such a large satisfaction, then our salvation must indeed be something considerable.

St. Paul's letters speak to us of this. He writes: "If anyone is in Christ, there is a new creation: everything old has passed away; see, everything has become new!" (2 Cor 5:17). Again and again the New Testament speaks to us of the riches that Christ has won for us through his sacrificial death. In the second letter to the Corinthians we also find: "For you know the generous act of our Lord Jesus Christ, that though he was rich, yet for your sakes he became poor, so that by his poverty you might become rich" (2 Cor 8:9).

The person who receives this threefold message emanating from Christ's atoning sacrificial death with the ears and eyes of faith will be filled with great gratitude and fidelity toward our crucified Lord. In such thankfulness and loyalty we attain the strength to walk with Christ the way of the cross in our own life and through both joy and sorrow to remain faithful, hopeful, and loving people.

MEDITATION

So many people no longer have any interest in what takes place on Good Friday and Easter. Their hearts are empty and their senses are confused. They abandon themselves to the undertow of the impulses bombarding them and come to grief in a whirlpool of foolish desires. They live only from one day to the next. They have always the same rhythm: colorless, meaningless—until one day they also bang their heads against a transom that makes of their lives a living cross. Then they become indignant, bitter, despairing. . . .

Christianity does not evade the deepest questions life has to offer. In the shadows of Good Friday we can come before God with these questions. If our cross and our suffering become too heavy for us, we want to enter into combat even with God, to accuse God and to implore: "Why?"

Must Christians become despondent cross-bearers? No, for then what would become of the Good News! What Jesus desires is that we accompany him through the cross toward the light, to new life, to the resurrection. . . . Those who encounter the crucified Jesus can see through the darkness of suffering and death, and gradually will begin to understand things with their hearts that they cannot fully plumb with their understanding.

Philip Bosmans [1]

The Easter Vigil

LITURGICAL GUIDE

In the early Church, Holy Saturday was left without any liturgical celebration, if one excepts the Liturgy of the Hours that arose later. The faithful observed, as on Good Friday, a strict mourning fast with meditations on the death and burial of the Lord. During the Middle Ages a misguided liturgical development led to the anticipation of the celebration of the Easter vigil, the "mother of all vigils," early on the morning of Holy Saturday. In 1951 and 1955 Pope Pius XII restored the old code, which was taken over in the new Missal of 1970 and further tightened. On this Easter night "the Church keeps watch, awaiting the resurrection of Christ and celebrating it in the sacraments. The entire celebration of this vigil should take place at night, beginning after nightfall and ending with dawn" (General Norms 21).

The liturgy of the Easter vigil is divided into the service of light, the liturgy of the word, the celebration of baptism, and the Easter Eucharist. The light celebration begins with the blessing of the fire, the lighting of the Easter candle, and its joyful entrance into the church. During this entrance the priest (or deacon) three times lifts high the Easter candle as a symbol of the resurrected Lord and sings "Christ our light" *(Lumen Christi)*, to which the congregation responds "thanks be to God." Those present at the celebration then light their own candles from the Easter candle, and the priest or deacon sings the solemn Easter hymn, the *Exultet.*

The liturgy of the word then consists of seven Old Testament readings with a responsorial psalm and a prayer after each. They may be reduced to three; if this is done, however, the reading about the crossing of the Red Sea must be included, for it is a foreshadowing of the paschal mystery and baptism. The eighth reading is a pericope from the letter to the Romans (Rom 6:3-11), after which a festive "alleluia" is added to the responsorial psalm. The Gospel is the resurrection account from one of the three synoptics, following the annual cycle.

The celebration of baptism is planned so that, in the case of the baptism of adults, the sacrament of confirmation will also be administered (if no bishop is present, then by a priest empowered to do so). Even if there are no baptisms, there is a consecration of the baptismal water (for the Easter season) or at least a blessing of Easter water. At this point the entire congregation, holding their lighted candles, renew their baptismal promises. The priest sprinkles the congregation with the blessed water and pronounces, or rather leads, the Easter petitions.

The Easter Eucharist, with a special Preface and texts substituted in Eucharistic Prayers 1–3, concludes with a festive formal blessing and a dismissal embellished with a double "alleluia."

Spiritual Reflection

I have often concelebrated the liturgy of the Easter vigil. Year after year, however, the symbolism of the entrance of the Easter candle overwhelms me anew. It is like a sermon without words. I will here attempt to supply words of interpretation for this wordless homily.

The Easter candle lighted from the Easter fire is carried at the head of a small procession into the church. The great room is still in darkness. Is not this darkness already a powerful symbol? Do not many of our contemporaries live "in darkness and the shadow of death"? Is there not a darkness of hopelessness, despondency, and despair? Does not the darkness of the grave, into which we have lowered so many of our friends and relatives, oppress us?—the darkness of the grave, in which the Lord himself has remained since Good Friday?

Now the deacon hoists high the burning Easter candle and sings "Christ our light." Christ, the true light who illumines every person, has come into the world. "To his own he came, but his own did not accept him." More than that: they placed him on a cross, they tried to extinguish the "light of the world" because they loved darkness more than the light. However, this light is eternal light. People can close their eyes before it, but they cannot extinguish it.

The small procession with the light of Christ proceeds farther: the community joins with it in spirit. Who is not struck by Christ's words: "I am the light of the world. Whoever follows me will never walk in darkness but will have the light of life" (John 8:12). A further image from years long ago bursts to life: the people of God of the old covenant had left the land of slavery behind them. By night a pillar of fire went before them and showed them the way to freedom in the promised land.

A second time the procession pauses, a second time comes the intonation: "Christ our light." And now priest and ministers light their candles from the Easter candle. They pass on the light of Christ to those standing around them, as these do to their neighbors. Gradually the entire church is transformed into a sea of light, lit up to the farthest corners with hundreds of candles, all blazing with the one light of Christ. All individually carry Christ's light in their hands, but together they make up the one body of Christ, illuminated by his light, animated by his vital energy. The early Church clothed those newly baptized on this holy evening with white garments and called them "enlightened." It was the time when pagans said of Christians: "They shine like stars on a dark night. See how they love one another."

When the procession with the Easter candle has reached the sanctuary, it stops. The deacon turns to the congregation and sings for a third time "Christ our light." The Easter candle now shines between him and the congregation, Christ in the midst of his community. "Where two or three are gathered in my name, I am there among them" (Matt 18:20). And this remains true during the entire Easter period: for fifty days the Easter candle sheds its joyous light upon the community and thereby makes visible symbolically the mystery of our observances: Christ as light and life, as the high priest of the new covenant in the midst of his community. He who has emerged from the darkness of the grave and ascended to the glory of the Father is in our midst and through his apostle calls to us: "once you were darkness, but now in the Lord you are light. Live as children of light—for the fruit of the light is found in all that is good and right and true" (Eph 5:8-9).

What does our world, and what do our fellow humans need more urgently than goodness, justice, and truth? We are all summoned by the entrance of this Easter candle to advance and spread this light of Christ. In the Sermon on the Mount Jesus himself challenges us to this: "let your light shine before others, so that they may see your good works and give glory to your Father in heaven" (Matt 5:16).

MEDITATION

I beseech you, O powerful angels
Who burst open the rock tomb on Easter morning,
burst also the harder stone
of a love that has grown cold! O horrid chasms!

For Christ was once again condemned to death
and lies entombed in the cold death chambers
of a lost world.—
Come near, I beseech you, O mighty angels,
and wake the buried Christ!—

But the angels kept their luminous silence.
Finally one bowed down to embrace me with gentle wings
and whispered softly in my ear:
No, you wake him up, child,

Spirit together with the efforts of faithful disciples may accomplish there exists a stupendous model, on which our parish communities may look only with amazement and a holy envy: the first community of disciples in Jerusalem, which we might call the first parish in the history of the Church. We here encounter a spiritual attitude and practical posture that has become a compelling model for all later Christian communities. The Acts of the Apostles tells us about it, especially in the second and fourth chapters.

This early community was "of one heart and soul" (Acts 4:32). In place of egoism there reigned a willingness for mutual help based on authentic love that showed itself to the extent that people even sold their own property in order to put the proceeds at the disposal of those who were suffering from want. "They devoted themselves to the apostles' teaching" (Acts 2:42a). This was the guiding line in all matters of belief and life, in contrast to the way of speaking that is so common today, according to which it does not matter much what one believes, if only one is a decent person. They also freely gave their testimony about the apostolic belief to their fellow citizens: "They . . . spoke the word of God with boldness" (Acts 4:31).

The filling station for such unity, readiness to help, fidelity to the faith, and apostolic witness was participation in the liturgy: "They devoted themselves . . . to the breaking of bread and the prayers" (Acts 2:42b); "day by day . . . they spent much time together in the Temple" (Acts 2:46). It is no wonder that such a community exerted a strong power of attraction without any high-pressure salesmanship or sophisticated public relations strategy. The Acts of the Apostles describes them "praising God and having the goodwill of all the people. And day by day the Lord added to their number those who were being saved" (Acts 2:47).

While we admire this early model of a community of Christians, we are struck by the realization that the Church of our own days is quite distant from such a high level of faith and of love. The Russian Orthodox writer Tatiana Goricheva, who has lived for many years in the West, sums up the condition of the western Church in these words: "In spite of its strenuous attempt to stay abreast of current trends, the Church in the West is losing more people every day. It is as if the Spirit and its power had abandoned it."

It is certainly not because of any lack of power and willingness on the part of the divine Spirit, which indeed is identical with God's eternal love, that things are not going well in our time where the reign of God is concerned. Rather, the causes must be sought in a deficit on the human side. On the one hand, not a few spiritual and cultural developments within human society certainly have had a negative effect and hamper fervent Christian faith. On the other hand, many baptized Christians all too readily expose themselves to the many ideologies of our time that are opposed to God, and allow themselves to become infected by them. Also, many well-meaning Christians, caught up in a frenzy of activity and industrious careerism, seem to forget that prayer for divine strength is indispensable if God's reign is really to be established. The important sentence in the contemporary Pentecost sequence is overlooked:

> Where you are not, man has naught,
> Nothing good in deed or thought,
> Nothing free from taint of ill.

Only when God's Holy Spirit dwells within the human heart can work on behalf of God's reign succeed. However, God's grace must be prayed for, as our ancient wisdom and experience confirm. May the feast of Pentecost bestow on all of us a powerful incentive toward more zealous prayer for the light and power of the divine Spirit.

MEDITATION

The world does not renew itself all by itself; it renews itself only through human effort. New people are people with a new outlook, a new spirit and a new heart; it is they who will fashion the forms and structures in which a life that is again worthy of human beings can be lived. As long as this insight has not become the insight of all people in all countries, as long as people believe that a sick world can really be healed by external means alone, we will only be treating the symptoms and leaving the roots of our disease alone. . . .

Let no one say "I will put off this task until someone else takes the first step." Each of us must begin in our own heart and our own life. Each of us is called, and if we are all convinced and penetrated by the idea that it depends on me, then "it" will take care of itself. At many different points candles will be lit, and these will overcome the darkness and the cold of this hour. Let us believe in the word of the individual, in the value of a small number, and in the value of what is closest to us—from these comes the salvation of the world.

And it is here that Pentecost inserts its message. . . . Anyone who prays to the Holy Spirit asks for a renewal of heart so that it may be attuned to what God wants of us, that in the Holy Spirit we may understand and do what is right, that the love that is the interior love of God become a person in its own right may become the law of their lives and thereby ever more the fundamental law of the world.

In its spirit and heart, humankind encounters God's Holy Spirit. It is here that even today uncountable hidden miracles of renewal may occur. Who says that a Pentecost is no longer possible today? All time is God's time. God's Spirit is hovering over the waters of our world, too. We do not believe in the world's decline; we believe in a new beginning.

Heinrich Fries[8]

Source Notes, Part 3

1. Philip Bosmans, *Gelöster leben* (Freiburg: Herder, 1989) 35ff.

2. Gertrud von le Fort, *Hymnen an die Kirche* (Munich: Kösel, 1936) 98–99.

3. "Christ the Lord is Risen Again," words by Michael Weisse (1480–1534), tr. Catherine Winkworth (1827–1878), alt. *The Hymnal 1982* no. 184.

4. P. de la Tour du Pin, *Une lutte pour la vie,* N.R.F. (Paris: Gallimard, 1970) 296; quoted in Robert Gantoy and Romain Swaeles, eds., *Days of the Lord* 3, translated by Greg LaNave and Donald Molloy (Collegeville: The Liturgical Press, 1993) 75.

5. Johannes Pinsk, *Die Kraft des Gotteswortes* (Düsseldorf: Patmos, 1964) 272–73.

6. Alfred Bengsch, *Der Glaube an die Auferstehung* (Berlin: Thomas-Morus-Verlag, 1962) 130–31.

7. Romano Guardini, *The Lord,* translated by Elinor Castendyk Briefs (Chicago: Henry Regnery, 1954), 430. The words in brackets were omitted in the English translation.

8. Heinrich Fries, *Von der Partnerschaft Gottes. Wir sind nicht allein* (Freiburg, Basel, and Vienna: Herder, 1975) 50.

Solemnities of the Lord
in Ordinary Time

2:14-18) sees in Jesus' incarnation the condition for his office of high priest. The child in the Temple will later become the sacrificial lamb for all of humanity (prayer over the gifts).

SPIRITUAL REFLECTION

The new covenant that God has sealed with humanity through Christ emerges from the old as a tree grows from its root. For that reason it is understandable that we encounter, especially in the stories of Jesus' childhood, many Old Testament customs and instructions. Thus also in the Gospel for this feast Joseph and Mary bring Jesus to the Temple in Jerusalem on the fortieth day after his birth. Mary intends to carry out the customary "offering for purification," while at the same time she will present Jesus as the firstborn in the Temple and redeem him through a sacrifice. According to the law of Moses, a firstborn boy was considered God's property and was destined for Temple service. When later the Levites took over the service in the Temple this directive lost its force; still, a firstborn had to be redeemed through a monetary payment for the support of the priests.

Mary fulfilled these Old Testament prescriptions out of obedience to the Law. Because of the angel's message she realized that her Jesus belonged in a special way to God as Son of the Most High and as the Messiah of the world. So she left him free for his messianic service, resolved, as the handmaid of the Lord, also to prepare him for his future path through her maternal service.

During this presentation of Jesus in the Temple there develops a noteworthy encounter with a man named Simeon. He was evidently at an advanced age, but the Holy Spirit had revealed to him that before his death he would gaze on the Messiah. Illumined by the Spirit, Simeon now recognizes in this child Jesus the promised Messiah. He takes the child into his arms and utters a grateful blessing of praise, which has been called the night prayer of his life. Therein he describes Jesus as salvation for all peoples, a light for the Gentiles, and the glory of Israel. Here once again explodes the brilliance of the proclamation we have encountered at Christmas. Here the hopes of centuries and millenia, and not just for the aged Simeon, have been fulfilled: "A light of revelation to the nations, and the glory of your people, Israel," as the alleluia verse joyously puts it.

However, from the mouth of the same Simeon we learn that this Christ will also become a sign of contradiction. Whoever hears his words must take a position, must decide for himself or herself either for or against him. He came into this world as "the true light, which enlightens everyone" (John 1:9). However, the world did not know or recognize him. "He came to what was his own, and his own people did not accept him" (John 1:11) as later the prologue to the Fourth Gospel sums up the situation. With these words of Simeon, the shadow of Golgotha already begins to fall across the threshold of the new covenant.

Mary, his mother, will especially suffer from this rejection and hostility. Simeon's prophetic gaze also discerns her suffering and forewarns: "you yourself shall be pierced with a sword." Just as the earthly path of her Son will not be a triumphal march, but rather the way of the cross, so she also will have to walk a path of sorrow. In this way, just a few weeks after his birth, the mother of the Lord is drawn into the mystery of the cross. We may rightly suspect that Mary kept in her heart this prophetic word about a sword of suffering and turned it over often in her reflections.

All of us, however, should realize that we are also implicated. For we are all drawn into the prophecy that Jesus would be the occasion for the rise and fall of many. Today Jesus is still a sign of contradiction who calls for a decision.

We should gratefully recognize that, as "a revealing light to the Gentiles," Christ has called us into communion with himself through faith and baptism; he has also illumined us. Now the lines from the letter to the Ephesians apply to us as well: "for once you were darkness, but now in the Lord you are light. Live as children of light" (Eph 5:8). The light that has been bestowed upon us, however, must become a light for other people. We did not receive it just for ourselves. The Sermon on the Mount makes this clear in its first chapter: "You are the light of the world. A city built on a hill cannot be hid . . . let your light shine before others, so that they may see your good works and give glory to your Father in heaven" (Matt 5:14, 16). One does not have to be a pessimist to become alarmed at the widespread darkness, lack of direction, mistakes and confusion in our society. Every possible form of false light, even down to the silliest superstitions, flickers through our time as well. Do not Christ's words spring to mind: "I have compassion for the crowd"? The love of neighbor should also impel us to pass on Christ's light wherever and however it is possible for us to do so.

MEDITATION

A very noble figure, the aged Simeon! Through many, many years he had desired the Messiah's coming. Now with the unquestioning faith of a child, he adores Israel's hope in a workman's needy child. His glowing love causes him to feel young again as he takes the infant in his arms. There is nothing more he wants from life. Having seen the Redeemer, he is overcome with gratitude and pours out from his soul the night prayer of his life . . .

His beautiful canticle, the *Nunc dimittis,* has been incorporated into the Church's official night prayer (Compline), where it serves as an expression of thanksgiving for the graces and blessings of another day of redemption. As we sing it we see Simeon holding the child Jesus in his arms and then, with grateful heart, retiring from his earthly service to God. We, too, are in the Lord's service. At the close of day we hold the Savior in our arms, mystically speaking . . . Fervently we thank God for his blessings; and we are prepared, if it be his will, to take our leave from the world. Yes, Lord, now you may dismiss me, your servant. For with the eyes of faith I have again seen my Savior, Jesus. . . . How beautiful would Simeon's prayer fall from the lips of the dying; it would be the night prayer to life.

Pius Parsch [1]

The Annunciation of the Lord
(March 25)

LITURGICAL GUIDE

In the East by the middle of the sixth century there is evidence of the celebration of the Annunciation of the Lord on March 25, that is, nine months before Christ's birth. Besides "Annunciation of the Lord," it is also occasionally called "the Annunciation to Mary." Because of its eminent significance in the history of salvation, the new General Norms chose the first designation, and therefore list it among the solemnities of the Lord, without thereby intending to slight Mary's role in this sacred event. Should this feast fall during Holy Week or Easter Week, it is transferred to the Monday after the Easter octave.

Central to what is distinctive to the Mass is, of course, the pericope about the annunciation (Luke 1:26-38). What is here announced is the inbreaking of a new era, the beginning of the events that concern Christ. The customary texts of the Mass for this feast take up this incident. In Mary is fulfilled the sign of Immanuel from the Old Testament reading (Isa 7:10-14). The communion verse also refers to this. The second reading (Heb 10:4-10) spans the arc from Christ's "coming into the world" (cf. also the opening verse) to his paschal mystery. The gospel acclamation joyfully proclaims the mystery of this feast in the words of John's prologue (John 1:14): "The Word of God became man and lived among us; and we saw his glory." The special Preface gratefully praises this "realization of all hope" and sees therein the fulfillment of the ancient promise to Israel.

With faith in the mystery of Christ's incarnation the Church, recognizing therein its own origin (prayer over the gifts), asks that God may bestow upon it a share in the divine life of the Son (opening prayer), and "that by the power of his resurrection [we may] come to eternal joy" (concluding prayer).

This celebration has also sunk deep roots within popular piety in the form of songs and prayers. The Angelus prayer, which developed into its present form between the thirteenth and sixteenth centuries, merits special mention.

SPIRITUAL REFLECTION

The solemnity of the Annunciation of the Lord is a Christmas celebration outside the Christmas cycle. Since the sixth or seventh century the Church in both East and West has celebrated on March 25 Christ's taking on human flesh in Mary's womb. The biblical foundation is the text of Luke 1:26-38. The event described there constitutes one of the most important moments in salvation history, a profoundly significant instant. We can without exaggeration speak of a pivotal moment in the history of humankind, that is, of an event from which a unique blessing descended upon the entire human race.

The initiator of this pivotal moment is the almighty God of love who redeems the ancient promise by sending to God's people, and through them to all humankind, the expected Messiah, the "Immanuel" (God with us), the ruler and Savior of the world. God, who loves humankind, will not accomplish this act of redemption without humankind itself. For that purpose God has chosen a young maiden from Nazareth by the name of Mary. Her free selection is simultaneously her unique grace through God. Appropriately, the angel greets her with the words: "Rejoice, O highly favored daughter! The Lord is with you. Blessed are you among women." To the fearful Mary comes the divine message through the angel's mouth. Its content is nothing less than

God's offer of salvation to all humankind. "You shall conceive and bear a son and give him the name Jesus. Great will be his dignity and he will be called Son of the Most High. The Lord God will give him the throne of David his father. He will rule over the house of Jacob forever and his reign will be without end."

Bernard of Clairvaux, in a homily in praise of the Virgin, shows the whole world kneeling at the feet of Mary, awaiting her response to the angel's invitation:

> Why do you delay, why are you afraid? Believe, give praise, and receive. Let humility be bold, let modesty be confident. This is no time for virginal simplicity to forget prudence. In this matter alone, O prudent Virgin, do not fear to be presumptuous. Though modest silence is pleasing, dutiful speech is now more necessary. Open your heart to faith, O blessed Virgin, your lips to praise, your womb to the Creator. See, the desired of all nations is at your door, knocking to enter. If he should pass by because of your delay, in sorrow you would begin to seek him afresh, the One whom your soul loves. Arise, hasten, open. Arise in faith, hasten in devotion, open in praise and thanksgiving.[2]

With her "yes," Mary has flung open the door to the messianic era, for with her willingness to become the mother of the promised Messiah the miracle of the incarnation may take place within her womb: "The Word became flesh and lived among us" (John 1:14). Truly this was a pivotal moment in human history.

One can only contemplate this event with amazement, reverence, and strong faith. The key to access in faith is given by Luke 1:37: "nothing will be impossible with God." If a person admits as possible only what lies within the sphere of human experience, that person blocks his or her own path to this unique event in the history of the world. Such a one responds "no" to the creator of heaven and earth, who in this event reveals "the beauty of [divine] power," to use the words of the alternative opening prayer. The person, however, who says "yes" to this loving divine omnipotence may admit this event of salvation in unconditional faith and Christmas joy.

We owe gratitude not only to the originator of this pivotal moment, but also to the "servant of the Lord." As the representative of all humankind she has opened the door to God's gift of salvation. Far removed from all arrogance and false illusion, she became the first tabernacle on this earth, the first person to carry Christ. Her thoughts, her cares, and her sufferings were all for the one who was salvation for her and for us. What she did and suffered for Jesus, she does and suffers as well for you and me. Hence it is fitting and appropriate for our thoughts to remain with her for a while, that the angel's greeting return again and again on our lips and in our hearts: "Hail Mary, full of grace, the Lord is with you."

Therefore it is understandable that since the sixteenth century the Catholic branch of Christianity has loved the Angelus prayer that joins the narrative of the annunciation with three Hail Marys: "The angel of the Lord declared unto Mary . . ." And it was really no exaggerated folk piety when our ancestors, as the vesper bells chimed, interrupted their work and, in the prayer of the "angel of the Lord," brought to expression their grateful union with Mary and her divine child. May also in our time, which one often hears described as a "winter" for the Church, the petition of the concluding prayer be fulfilled: "strengthen our faith and hope in Jesus, born of a virgin and truly God and man."

MEDITATION

In the blink of an eye, which nevermore passes away,
but remains valid for all eternity,
your word became the word of all humanity,
your "yes," all creation's "amen" to God's "yes."
In faith and in your womb you conceived him who,
as both divine and human, creator and creation,
is changeless, fateless bliss
and the bitter, death-condemned fate
of this earth,
Jesus Christ our Lord.
For our salvation you said "yes."
You delivered this fiat on our behalf
as a woman of our own race.
For us you took up
and hid in your womb and in your love
him in whose name alone
there is salvation on earth and in heaven.
Your "yes" holds firm forever.
It has never been rescinded—
not even when it became clear
in the course of the life and death of your Son
exactly who he was whom you conceived:
the Lamb of God
who took upon himself the sins of the world.

Karl Rahner[3]

Trinity Sunday

LITURGICAL GUIDE

The threat posed by the Arian heresy, which was formally condemned in the councils of Nicea (325) and Constantinople (381), led to a distinctive emphasis on the preaching and devotional practice of trinitarian belief in the lands of Spain and Gaul, which were particularly affected by this error. There thus appeared in the middle of the eighth century in the ancient Gelasian sacramentary the Preface we have today for this feast, a sharpened, abbreviated version of the classical doctrine of the Trinity. In 800 a votive Mass in honor of the Trinity appeared as a Sunday Mass. We have evidence of a special feast in the Benedictine monasteries in the land of the Franks and in Gaul before the end of the millennium. Rome hesitated a long while before instituting such a solemnity, for the simple reason that each Sunday contains a memorial of the Trinity. It was Pope John XXII who inaugurated this feast for the whole Church in the year 1334.

The celebration is held on the Sunday after Pentecost as a kind of grateful review of the now completed mystery of salvation, which the Father has accomplished through the Son in the Holy Spirit. The scriptural readings, including the responsorial psalm, are different in all three annual cycles, so that thereby an inclusive range of the kerygma may be brought before the community. As to the common texts, the opening verse begins with a praise of the three-personed God who has shown such love for us. The opening and concluding prayers ask that we may preserve correct belief that allows us to recognize and honor the Trinity. The gospel acclamation consists in the doxology: "Glory to the Father . . ."

In year A the Gospel (John 3:16-18) proclaims the love of God that has sent the Son for the salvation of the world. The New Testament reading (2 Cor 13:11-13) promises this "God of love and peace." In the Old Testament reading (Exod 34:4b, 5-6, 8), God is revealed as merciful, gracious, patient, and rich in kindness and fidelity.

In year B the Gospel brings the concluding section of Matthew with the great commission, which names the three divine persons in connection with baptism. The Old Testament reading (Deut 4:12-14, 39-40) emphasizes the uniqueness and unity of YHWH, while the New Testament reading from the letter to the Romans (Rom 8:14-17) announces the grace of those who are children of God through the Spirit, through which we have become heirs of God and co-heirs with Christ.

The Gospel of year C (John 16:12-15) directs our gaze to the interior trinitarian life of God: the Spirit glorifies the Son by proclaiming what the Son is, who together with the Father possesses all things. The Old Testament reading (Prov 8:22-31) sings the praise of divine Wisdom; this is seen as an allusion to God's multiple personhood. The New Testament reading (Rom 5:1-5) proclaims peace with God through Christ. Our hope in God's glory is founded in God's love, which is poured into our hearts through the Holy Spirit.

SPIRITUAL REFLECTION

When Edith Stein became a Catholic in 1932 she went to Breslau to visit her mother, who was firmly rooted in her Jewish faith. When she said to her, "Mother, I have become a Catholic," her mother wept in sorrow over her daughter's apparent betrayal of her Jewish faith. Edith remained with her several months and accompanied her to synagogue services just as before. On one occasion as the rabbi read out the words "Hear, O Israel, the Lord is One," her mother whispered to her: "You see? God is only one."

For Jews and Moslems the Christian teaching of one God in three persons is an offensive stumbling block. They see in this a violation of the belief in one God. Other "believers" reject the Christian doctrine of the trinitarian nature of God because they consider it contrary to reason.

How do we Christians actually arrive at this belief, which is and remains for us also an impenetrable mystery? We do so because the New Testament scriptures that rest on Jesus Christ proclaim it in numerous places as God's revelation, and this with unmistakable clarity. We will only quote one sentence from Jesus' own mouth: "I will ask the Father, and he will give you another Advocate, to be with you forever" (John 14:16). For humans, God lives in unapproachable light, as Scripture tells us. But of Jesus the Fourth Gospel says: "No one has ever seen God. It is God the only Son, who is close to the Father's heart, who has made him known" (John 1:18).

This report of Jesus Christ teaches us that the creator of the heavens and the earth is no impersonal "highest essence," no heartless "ultimate condition of the cosmos," but rather a loving Father from whom his co-equal Son comes forth from all eternity, just as bright light has poured forth from the sun's furnace since its beginning. From the two of them, however, because the love between them is so strong that it has become a person in its own right, the Holy Spirit proceeds. Because, according to their deepest nature, these three divine persons are love, this also streams forth onto us humans and transforms us through Christ's redeeming work into children of the trinitarian God.

The belief in the three-personed God is common to all Christians. When the Pope visited Germany in the autumn of 1980 he received representatives from all the other Christian churches and denominations in the cathedral of Mainz. To make visible the unity of Christians, an ecumenical commission was then set up in order to explore and prepare ways toward the reunification of separated Christians.

The first fruit of these efforts was a statement by all ten Christian denominations on Pentecost in 1981. The occasion was the 1600th anniversary of the Council of Constantinople (381) and its famous creed, which was solemnly promulgated at this and the previous Council of Nicea (325). "In this creed the Church confessed who this God is in whom Christians believe and in whom we place our trust in both life and death." This common declaration of all ten denominations makes clear that this creed is binding upon all Christianity in its Eastern and Western expressions, in the Roman Catholic and Reformed traditions, and is deeper than anything that divides them. Its exact words are: "This mutually acknowledged truth of the gospel shows that the division between our Churches does not reach to the roots. A common confession of the trinitarian God is the indispensable condition for the unity of the one, holy, catholic, and apostolic Church."

We will quote three fundamental sentences from this important declaration that briefly outline the trinitarian belief:

1. With the Nicene creed we believe and confess that the Almighty, the creator of heaven and earth, who from all eternity is the Father of Jesus, is also our Father.

2. With the Nicene creed we believe and confess that in the person of Jesus Christ, God himself became truly human, and that in the life and death of this one person from the people of Israel God is present for all human beings.

3. With the Nicene creed we believe and confess that in the Holy Spirit God himself comes into our hearts and is active among us in liberating words and deeds.[4]

Such a commonality is ground for rejoicing and is well suited to strengthening us in our belief in the trinitarian God. However, it is important that we not only speak about God, but speak to God, that is, that we pray to God. Prayer is able to lead us deeper into this mystery and to drive away all doubt:

If human eyes are to see, heaven must open itself and a beam from its light penetrate our dark heart. Recognition is the inheritance not of the wise, but of the devout; not from brooding, but from praying will you receive revelation.

(W. Weber)[5]

Prayer leads us simultaneously to a stronger rootedness and familiarity with the God who is three in one and gives us the strength to do the will of God and to cooperate in the building up of God's reign.

MEDITATION

As the only-begotten Son of God,
our Lord and God Jesus Christ,
through whom everything was made, calls out:
"I have come down from heaven
not to do my own will,
but the will of the Father who sent me" . . .
and as the Holy Spirit, who distributes the great
and wonderful gifts, and is at work in all things,
says nothing of himself, but rather speaks what
he hears from the Father, how much more should
not the whole Church exert itself to preserve
the unity of the Spirit within the bonds of peace,
and to fulfill the words of the Acts of the Apostles:
"The whole group of those who believed were of one heart and soul,"
because no one pursued his or her own will,
but rather all together sought in the one Holy Spirit
the will of the one Lord Jesus Christ,
who said: "I have come down from heaven,
not to do my own will,
but the will of the Father who sent me,"
and who says to the Father:
"I ask not only on behalf of these, but also on behalf of those
who will believe in me through their word,
that they may all be one."

Basil of Caesarea (d. 379)

The Body and Blood of Christ (Corpus Christi)

LITURGICAL GUIDE

The institution of the sacrament of the Eucharist on Holy Thursday must be ranked as one of Christ's principal acts of salvation. However, it was not until the thirteenth century that it received its own feast (in German called *Fronleichnam*, "the body of the Lord"). The reasons for the initiation of the feast were, on the one hand, the growing veneration for the sacrament of the Eucharist in the twelfth and thirteenth centuries, and on the other hand the fact that the memorial on Holy Thursday at the beginning of Passiontide scarcely permitted a festive celebration with singing and rejoicing. The festival was first celebrated in the mid-thirteenth century in the diocese of Liège. A few decades later we have reports of a Corpus Christi procession.

If contemporary folk piety as well as that of the following centuries tended to isolate Christ's presence in the form of the Eucharist, it is still true that the bull *Transiturus* (Urban IV, 1264) establishing the feast, and the liturgical texts, which were in large part written by Thomas Aquinas, happily emphasize the inclusive dimension of this sacrament as a memorial of the paschal mystery that simultaneously makes it present. In the interest of this more comprehensive view the earlier official name, "Feast of the Most Holy Body of Christ," was changed to "Solemnity of the Body and Blood of Christ." It then also became clear that the "Feast of the Precious Blood" (introduced in 1849) is also contained in Corpus Christi and, being a repetition, should be dropped.

The proper of the Mass has different readings and responsorial psalms in the three yearly cycles, but the customary texts remain the same. The prayers of the presider allow the authorship of Thomas Aquinas, drawing upon his theological *Summa*, to be recognized clearly: from the perspective of the past, the Eucharist is a memorial of the paschal mystery (opening prayer), from the perspective of the present, "unity and peace" are its interior fruits (prayer over the gifts), and in looking toward the future, it is the "foretaste of the life to come" (concluding prayer).

We encounter Thomas's classical theology also in the sequence *Lauda, Sion, Salvatorem* (cf. "Zion, Praise thy Savior,"[6] and the German hymns *Deinem Heiland* and *Lobe, Zion, deinen Hirten*). The gospel acclamation brings Christ's words about the living bread, which guarantees everlasting life (cf. John 6:51).

Of the scriptural readings, only the Gospels from the three cycles will be briefly sketched here: in year A the Gospel is taken from John's account of the eucharistic promise (John 6:51-58); in year B the Gospel describes Jesus' last supper (Mark 14:12-16, 22-26); the Gospel for year C recounts the miracle of the multiplication of loaves as a clear reference to the eucharistic meal (Luke 9:11b-17).

Either of the two eucharistic Prefaces may be chosen; both interpret the salvific significance of this sacrament as a memorial that makes present the sacrifice of the cross and the banquet that brings salvation.

SPIRITUAL REFLECTION

The people of God of the old covenant discovered that they could not survive the long journey and stay in the wilderness without God's help. God often came to their rescue at the moment of greatest need. It was God who, according to the first reading (year A), "guided you through the vast and terrible desert with its saraph serpents and scorpions, its parched and waterless ground; who brought forth water for you from the flinty rock and fed you in the desert with manna" (Deut 8:15-16a).

The people of God of the new covenant also recognize themselves in many respects as embarked on a dangerous pilgrimage. It is said that we are only guests on the earth and wander without rest through all sorts of hardships toward our eternal home. On this pilgrimage God gives us helpful guidance through the Son. In the words of a hymn, "one alone accompanies us, the Lord Christ; he walks faithfully at our side when everything else fails us." He does this also and most especially through the sacrament we refer to through its Greek name, "Eucharist," the sacrament of giving thanks. Christ himself explained the importance of this great deed of salvation in his preaching at Capernaum: "He who feeds on my flesh and drinks my blood has life eternal, and I will raise him up on the last day. . . . The man who feeds on my flesh and drinks my blood remains in me, and I in him . . . the man who feeds on me will have life because of me" (John 6:54-55). It is the sacrament of his body offered for us and of his blood poured out for us.

If it is true that in the folk piety of previous centuries Christ's presence was regarded as restricted to the specific piece of bread, the Church documents and the liturgical texts of this celebration, the latter primarily from Thomas Aquinas, emphasize the universal dimensions of the sacrament: the actualization of the sacrificial death and resurrection of the Lord as the congregation confesses it during the Mass after the words of consecration: "When we eat this bread and drink this cup, we proclaim your death, Lord Jesus, until you come in glory."

This solidarity with Christ's paschal mystery should obviously not remain only a confession on our lips, but rather should lead us into a harmony with the love of Christ serving and offering itself for others. The most profound attitude of the Lord must also become that of his mystical body, constituted by all the baptized. This thought finds powerful expression in the new German hymn "The Grain of Wheat Must Die," which leads us to the center of the eucharistic mystery. The second stanza of this hymn says: "Thus the Lord gave up his life, gave himself like bread. Whoever receives this bread proclaims his death." However, this means that all those who participate in this celebration are themselves taken up by this mystery into the duty that is described in the next two stanzas:

> Who celebrate this mystery, themselves become like bread;
> they must let themselves be devoured by all human need.
> As bread for many people has Our Lord chosen us;
> We live for one another, and nothing counts but love.

In this way the eucharistic celebration develops into a deeply involving social obligation, the measure of our belief in and veneration of the holy body and blood of Christ. The participants in the Corpus Christi procession should also have this same outlook, for according to its deepest nature it should not consist in a triumphal victory march, which would be nothing more than a simple demonstration of our faith, but rather a symbolic expression of our pilgrim status as we traverse the deserts of this life, along which the Lord himself gives us directions and a protecting escort, and also takes us up into the obligation of his consuming love.

MEDITATION

Christ "for us"—that is his way of being in himself, but also the manner of his presence in the Eucharist: Christ is there wholly for us; his life belongs entirely to us; his life is given over wholly to us. The ground and source of this devotion is Christ's love. . . .

Our response must correspond to this "way of being for us." In that he gives himself up for us, "those who live . . . live no longer for themselves, but for him who died and was raised for them" (2 Cor 5:15). . . . Christ's "being for us" must become with us a "being for one another." The appropriate response to Christ's "for us" will be a new way of being "for each other." . . .

Those who attend Mass centered upon themselves and with their eyes only on what is their own, with their backs turned to their brothers and sisters, do not celebrate the Lord's Supper, but eat and drink judgment to themselves. For the apostles the eucharistic banquet was immediately and directly connected with Christ's principal command: "I give you a new commandment, that you love one another. Just as I have loved you, you also should love one another" (John 13:34). This transformation in love is our response to Christ's loving sacrifice (Eph 5:2). . . . Whoever would be great must serve the others; whoever would be first must become the servant of all (Matt 20:28). This is the challenge to which we must respond.

Theodor Schneider[7]

The Sacred Heart of Jesus

LITURGICAL GUIDE

This solemnity, which was made obligatory for the universal church only in 1856, is celebrated on the third Friday after Pentecost, the day that previously concluded the octave of Corpus Christi. It venerates the one divine and human Christ from the standpoint of his love for humankind, a love symbolized by his heart. It is therefore a devotional celebration that has as its object Christ's love for us rather than any specific salvific act.

The Mass for this feast in the new Missal largely takes over the text that Pius XI put forward in 1928, in which the notion of expiation is more prominent than before. The particulars of the Mass are different in the three yearly cycles, similar to the situation of Corpus Christi, with different scriptural readings and responsorial psalms for each cycle. There is also an alternative alleluia verse in years B and C.

The opening verse uses Psalm 33:11, 19 to invoke the decree of the Lord and "the thoughts of his heart," which are directed toward the salvation of our lives. There is a choice between two texts for the opening prayer. The first rejoices in the "gifts of love" received from the heart of Jesus; the second text, similar to the prayer over the gifts, gives expression to the notion of atonement. The concluding prayer asks for the gift of divine love so that we may recognize Christ in others. The texts offered for the communion verse give two quotations from the Fourth Gospel that have always played a special role in the long history of devotion to the Sacred Heart (John 7:37-38 and 19:34, describing

Jesus as the source of living waters and the scene of the piercing of Jesus' side). The new Preface is distinctive in its closeness to the holy Scriptures and to the theology of the Church Fathers.

The Gospel in cycle A (Matt 11:25-30) gives the joyful messianic call and Jesus' invitation to come to him for peace and to learn from his heart: "for I am gentle and humble of heart." The Gospel in cycle B describes how the lance pierced Jesus' side (John 19:31-37). The Church Fathers saw in the blood and water that poured forth the origin of the Church and its sacraments. The good shepherd who seeks out the lost sheep and carries it home on his shoulders full of joy (Luke 15:3-7) is the theme of the Gospel in year C. So in all their diversity the gospel texts still circle around one and the same theme: Jesus' heart is turned toward humanity.

Spiritual Reflection

When we hear the word "heart," we most often think of that organ, that ingeniously designed muscle, that is responsible for pumping blood throughout the body. From it all the arteries branch out, supplying the body down to the most minute vessels with the blood that is essential for life, and bringing it back to the heart for renewal. The heart is thus the life-preserving center of the organism. We hear often of people struck with various kinds of heart disease, or even with heart attacks or heart failure. Lucky the people with healthy hearts; they should be very grateful for them.

However, our language also uses the word "heart" in a more extended sense. We say of a good person that he or she has a good heart; such people have their hearts in the right place, have hearts full of love and compassion, or similar expressions. We thereby give high praise to their interior attitude and disposition, their character. In contrast, we sometimes speak of a person with no heart, a heart of stone, a heart without compassion, whereby we intend to pay the person no compliment. Thus the word "heart" in this extended sense refers to the innermost center of a person. For millennia it has provided this service in human language by referring to the whole person including his or her disposition and behavior.

It is in this extended sense that we speak in today's feast of the Sacred Heart of Jesus. Jesus' heart reaches out toward humankind. He does not put himself at a distance from people like some civil bureaucrat or severe judge, but rather is radically concerned about each one of us in heartfelt love. Even when a person has marched off defiantly and taken a wrong path, it is precisely at such moments that, like the good shepherd, Christ goes out in search of him or her. Like the good shepherd he carries his lost sheep home on his shoulders full of joy and calls out to his neighbors: rejoice with me, for I have found my sheep again, the one that was lost. Jesus himself uses the word in this extended sense when he says "I am gentle and humble of heart" (Matt 11:29). Being "humble of heart" means having a heart that is willing to serve. As he says on another occasion: "the Son of Man came not to be served but to serve, and to give his life a ransom for many" (Matt 20:28).

Thus we should not be surprised that even the early Church already revered the Lord's heart, which a soldier had pierced with a lance. In the high Middle Ages a veneration of Jesus developed under the symbol of his loving heart, out of which there flowed "rivers of living water" (John 7:38). Devotion to the Sacred Heart received particular force through the efforts of Margaret Mary Alacoque of the Order of the Visitation, to whom Christ appeared on many occasions, instructing her to work for the institution of a feast for the Sacred Heart, for the First Friday devotions to the Sacred Heart, and for the holy hour on the previous evening.

Certainly there was much hesitation and reservation, especially during the period of the so-called Enlightenment. Many felt offended by the paintings and plaster statues that were sometimes sentimental "kitsch." However, anyone who has understood that the veneration of the Sacred Heart is nothing else than the veneration of Christ under the symbol of his heart will be helped rather than offended and will be led to the personal center of Christian belief.

With our eyes on the heart of our Lord and also on our own often selfish heart that is incapable of true, enduring love, we may recall the prayer to the Sacred Heart in the German Catholic prayer book, *Gotteslob*: "O most sacred heart of Jesus, model our hearts on your own. Fill our hearts with kindness for all we meet; make us compassionate toward the sick and the disadvantaged, and ready to help anyone who has a heavy cross to bear. Keep our hearts free from every form of egoism, open or concealed. May our hearts strive to become messengers of your gospel and to smooth the path for your salvation, O redeemer of the world."[8]

MEDITATION

I am so tired of myself.
I become disheartened
when I dare to perceive

how much resistance is at home in my heart,
O my God, against you.
How much evil lurks in me,
even if much of it rarely breaks the surface,
how much indifference,
how much incapacity for a loving surrender.
Often I dream, O Lord,
of a new heart.
I would like a heart in myself
that loses itself entirely in you,
a heart that burns for you
and seeks to do your will,
a heart full of trust,
a heart that has room for the suffering,
that does not wall itself up from anxiety
but dares to accept its vulnerability
because it lives out of your saving love,
a heart that in the midst of clamor can hear your voice;
a heart in which your praise lives.
Let me not become too tired, my God,
to ask for such a heart from you.

Sabine Naegeli[9]

The Transfiguration
(August 6)

LITURGICAL GUIDE

We find a festival dedicated to the transfiguration for the first time
in the East Syrian Church in the fifth century, from which it was picked
up by the other Eastern churches. In the West we encounter it for the
first time in the tenth century in the Frankish-Roman Church. During
the period of the crusades it quickly spread to other regions. However,
it was not until 1457 that Pope Callixtus III introduced it for the entire
Church. The historical occasion for this was gratitude for the previous
year's victory over the Turks, by whom the West was severely threatened.

Naturally Christ's transfiguration stands at the center of the Mass for this day. The Gospel pericope is taken from one of the three synoptic gospels, corresponding to the yearly cycle. The mystery of this feast also echoes in the opening and alleluia verses, as well as in the second reading from the second letter of Peter (2 Pet 1:16-19). The first reading (Dan 7:9-10, 13-14) presents us with the vision of the "Ancient One" seated upon a fiery throne, and the appearance of "one like a son of man," to whom will be given dominion over the world; this vision is also reflected on in the responsorial psalm (verses from Psalm 97). The special Preface celebrates the significance of Christ's transfiguration in that it gives the disciples the power to carry their crosses and bestows upon them the hope of eternal transfiguration. The prayers for the eucharistic celebration ask that we may share in Christ's glory.

For the spiritual reflection and meditation, the reader is referred to the Second Sunday of Lent, whose Gospel is also that of the transfiguration.

The Triumph of the Cross
(September 14)

LITURGICAL GUIDE

The cross on which Christ died had already in the time of the apostles become the symbol of his sacrificial death, even a symbol for himself and the Christian faith. On September 13 in the year 335 the Church of the Martyrdom and Resurrection was dedicated in Jerusalem. On the day after, in a solemn ceremony, the faithful were shown the cross that the empress Helen had discovered on September 14, 320. This ceremony was later repeated in the church, which possessed a large relic of the cross, every year on September 14. The reverent elevation of the relic of the true cross gave this day its German name, *Kreuzerhöhung,* "exaltation of the cross." Later this feast was combined with the memorial of the rescue of the stolen cross from the Persians by the emperor Heraclius in the year 628.

At the center of the Mass for this day stands Christ's death on the cross and the redemption he thereby attained for us. Thus the opening verse says: "We should glory in the cross of our Lord Jesus Christ, for he is our salvation, our life and our resurrection; through him we are saved and made free" (cf. Gal 6:14). The special Preface compares the cross with the tree in the garden of Eden. That tree produced death for humankind, this tree life. As a model for the saving cross, the liturgical texts propose the "bronze serpent" that Moses formerly had "raised" on a pole in the wilderness and that bestowed healing on all who had been bitten by a serpent and were mortally ill, if they turned their gaze believingly upon it. The first reading (Num 21:4-9) reports this incident. In the same way eternal life proceeds from the Son of Man who has been raised up (John 3:13-17, the Gospel pericope). The second reading (Phil 2:6-11) presents the classic expression for Christ's humiliation "even to death on a cross" and his resurrection. The community responds in the alleluia verse with adoration and praise. The presider's prayers ask for "the gift of redemption" (opening prayer), freedom from sin (prayer over the gifts), and the glory of the resurrection (concluding prayer). These gifts of salvation are brought together in the communion verse in Christ's promise: "When I am lifted up from the earth, I will draw all men to myself" (John 12:32).

SPIRITUAL REFLECTION

As on Good Friday, so on this day the cross on Golgotha stands at the center of the liturgy. And yet the Mass for the feast of the Triumph of the Cross is fundamentally different from that on Good Friday. The latter, as the day of Christ's death and as the actualizing memorial of his terrible suffering and death, is marked by the deepest solemnity and compassion, and is accompanied by a sorrowful fasting. It is true that at one point in the veneration of the cross the joy of salvation bursts forth, when the antiphon says: "We worship you, Lord, we venerate Your cross, we praise your resurrection. Through the cross you brought joy to the world." However, immediately the sober and mournful *Improperia* resume ("My people, what have I done to you?") in which the deep tragedy of this event comes to expression. It is not possible for the joy over our salvation to come to the fore on Good Friday.

It is different on the feast of the "exaltation of the cross," which we should more properly call the "Triumph of the Cross" and that counts as another feast of a devotional-memorial character; it has a pronounced joyous character.

The ancient Romans had a proverb: *"Quotidiana velescunt"*: "what happens every day is not very important." With reference to the cross of Christ, do not we Christians stand in a similar situation? We see the cross so often, in so many different places: in church, in our room, in public displays and even on the tops of some mountains. Beyond that, we make the "sign of the cross" over ourselves before and after we pray. In the secular realm as well the word "cross" has experienced an almost inflationary usage: not only as a symbol of honor or service, as in the "Red Cross," "Iron Cross," and so on, but also in everyday terms such as "criss-cross," "crossword," and many other expressions. Is there not some danger that the symbol of Christian salvation may lose much of its significance? Is there some way to resist the tendency expressed in the Roman proverb?

A solution might be found if we allow ourselves to speak of the striking symbolism of the two beams that make up the cross: the upright (vertical) beam with its orientation pointing both above and below may remind us that the Son of God came down from heaven for us and for our salvation. It is thus a symbol of God's love for humankind, which shows itself especially in the incarnation and in Christ's sacrificial death on the cross. But the upright beam is also a reminder of the constant necessity of lifting up the human spirit to God: "To you, O God, we lift up our souls in confidence." If people give up this "upward climb" to God (transcendence), they quickly lose consciousness of their own creaturely status and therewith a fundamental dimension of their humanity. Then the illusion of human autonomy expands all too quickly, bringing error and confusion in its wake.

The horizontal (cross) beam points both left and right, and thereby indicates our fellow human beings. It reminds us that, together with the love of God, the love of neighbor belongs to the principal commandment for Christians. There is no true piety that overlooks or passes by our neighbor. "God and I" can never be the exclusive motto of Christian life. Christ himself demonstrated symbolically with his arms extended on the cross what before he had proclaimed: "when I am lifted up from the earth, I will draw all men to myself" (John 12:32), the communion verse of today's Mass. The author Christian Morgenstern made these words of Christ into the subject of a poem, to which he gave the telling title "The Cross":

> I have seen humankind in its humblest form,
> I have plumbed the world down to its most basic germ.
> I know that love, love is its deepest meaning,
> and that I am here so as to love ever more.
> I stretch my arms wide, just as HE has done,
> I would like to embrace, like HIM, the whole world.[10]

Christ's entire life was a being present for us, and specifically with reference to loving service (foot washing) he says also to us: "I have set you an example, that you also should do as I have done to you" (John 13:15). Thus I cannot really love God and Christ if I deny my fellow human beings practical love in concrete situations. Christ refers every good deed, but also every good deed left undone, to himself: "you did it (did not do it) to me" (cf. Matt 25:40, 45).

In this way the vertical and horizontal beams of the cross can become reminders of the principles of a Christian way of life, a sermon without words. Would this not be the most significant "exaltation" and "triumph" of the cross, if we were to give this symbol such a position in our lives? The feast of the Triumph of the Cross should remind us of this every year.

MEDITATION

The royal banners forward go,
the cross shines forth in mystic glow
where he through whom our flesh was made,
in that same flesh our ransom paid.

Fulfilled is all that David told
in true prophetic song of old;
how God the nations' King should be,
for God is reigning from the tree.

O tree of beauty, tree most fair,
ordained those holy limbs to bear
gone is thy shame, each crimsoned bough
proclaims the King of glory now.

Blest tree, whose chosen branches bore
the wealth that did the world restore,
the price which none but he could pay
to spoil the spoiler of his prey.

O cross, our one reliance, hail!
Still may thy power with us avail
to save us sinners from our sin,
God's righteousness for all to win.

To thee, eternal Three in One,
let homage meet by all be done;
as by the cross thou dost restore
so rule and guide us evermore.

Venantius Fortunatus (died c. 600) [11]

Anniversary of the Dedication of a Church

LITURGICAL GUIDE

The anniversary of the dedication of its own church occupies a prominent position in the life of every parish community. Originally the first celebration of the Eucharist counted as the dedication of a church building. A specific rite for the dedication of churches developed slowly in the Roman Church only after the seventh century. Its rich symbolic aspects have the purpose of making clear the value of the house of God and of the liturgies celebrated in it.

The texts of the Mass for this celebration are the same in all three yearly cycles. The Old Testament reading gives King Solomon's prayer at the dedication of the Temple he built in Jerusalem (1 Kgs 8:22-23, 27-30). The beautiful verses of the responsorial psalm (Psalm 84) give witness to the joy and security to be found in the Lord's house. The reading from the first letter of Peter (1 Pet 2:4-9) describes the community as a spiritual house built from "living stones," as a "holy priesthood" that brings forth "spiritual sacrifices" through Christ. The Gospel (John 2:13-22), following upon Jesus' cleansing of the Temple, reveals Christ as the true temple of the new covenant. This temple (his body) will be torn down, but he will rebuild it in three days. The communion verse (1 Cor 3:16) proclaims that the community—and thus also the individual Christian—is God's holy temple in which the divine Spirit lives. The special Preface widens the perspective from the physical building of a church as the place where the "pilgrim Church" assembles to the "temple of living stones" and the mystical body of Christ, and ascends to the "heavenly city of Jerusalem." The presider's prayers ask for the proper disposition during the religious service and the richness of God's saving love (opening prayer), that we ourselves become an acceptable offering to God (prayer over the gifts), and that through this solemn celebration of the Eucharist we may be transformed into "the temple of your presence" (concluding prayer).

SPIRITUAL REFLECTION

Every year our communities celebrate the anniversary of the dedication of their churches, full of grateful joy that a place has been made available for them to meet the triune God, a place of religious security and confident hope. It might well have been a similar state of mind that led the psalmist of the old covenant to sing:

> I was glad when they said to me, "Let us go to the house of the Lord!" (Ps 122:1).

> How lovely is your dwelling place, O Lord of hosts! My soul longs, indeed it faints for the courts of the Lord (Ps 84:1-2).

> For a day in your courts is better than a thousand elsewhere (Ps 84:10).

If we consult the New Testament, however, it becomes apparent that our Christian churches are not simply a continuation of the Temple of the Old Testament. Nowhere does the New Testament describe the place of religious assembly as a temple or house of God or a Holy of Holies. Rather, the temple of the new covenant is Christ himself, as the Gospel for this feast announces. He, the exalted Lord, is in his resurrected body the future location of God's saving presence. Anyone who is seeking God must look for God in Christ. In him are fulfilled his words to the Samaritan woman at Jacob's well: "but the hour is coming, and is now here, when the true worshipers will worship the Father in spirit and truth" (John 4:23). An encounter with the saving Lord is thus no longer restricted to a particular place, as it was earlier to the Temple in Jerusalem, but rather it occurs in our being united with Jesus. At his death the curtain in the Temple was torn in two (cf. Matt 27:51), which many of the Church Fathers interpret as indicating the end of the Temple cult of the old covenant and the beginning of a new order of salvation.

However not only Christ, but also the Christian community, the people of God of the new covenant, are described in the New Testament as the temple of God. Thus the communion verse for the feast of the dedication of a church: "You are the temple of God, and God's Spirit dwells in you. The temple of God is holy; you are that temple" (1 Cor 3:16-17). Everyone who is joined with Christ through faith and love builds up his mystical body (cf. 1 Cor 10:17; 12:27, and elsewhere). The love of the heavenly Father rests from now on not only on the Son, but also on all who are joined with the Son in faith through the Holy Spirit (John 16:27). Indeed, everyone who loves Jesus becomes a home to the triune God (cf. John 14:23).

The members of the mystical body of Christ are also compared in the New Testament to living stones that, laid one upon the other, soar up into a spiritual temple, as the second reading proclaims (1 Pet 2:4). We may take this as a context for understanding Christ's saying, "where two or three are gathered in my name, I am there among them" (Matt 18:20).

We can thus understand why the Christians of the first centuries did not have particular church buildings, but rather gathered together in their houses to hear the word of God, to pray, and to celebrate the Eucharist. Only as their numbers increased did the necessity for larger gathering places arise. For these there was no particular rite of consecration; rather, they received their status from the community that was joined with Christ and the Eucharist that was celebrated in them.

The later development of church construction ("church" is from the Greek words *kyriake oikia*, "house of the Lord;" this term was then transferred to refer to the community that assembled there) led gradually to a situation in which the physical church was taken as a symbol for the spiritual Church, and the architecture and decoration were developed correspondingly. Finally there also arose (beginning in the seventh century) a more comprehensive ritual of consecration whose parts were intended to symbolize the dignity of the Mass and the nobility of the community bound to Christ.

For all our joy over an artfully designed and carefully embellished church building, we should not overlook the fact that the "living stones" are indeed more important and more valuable than the material. What good are the most elegant churches if the temple of the Holy Spirit, as Paul calls Christians, is falling into disrepair through a lack of faith, hope, or charity? Over a hundred years ago, in his book *The Gay Science,* the philosopher of culture Friedrich Nietzsche accused the "madmen" who were flattering themselves that they had "murdered God" and with whom Nietzsche identified himself, of bringing about the "death of God." Such "mad" people have made their way into various churches and sung *requiem aeternam Deo* ("eternal rest for God"). Their basic critique, rendered explicit and public, is always the same: "What are these churches now if they are not the tombs and sepulchers of God?"

Is it possible to utter such blasphemies about our churches as Nietzsche did with these words? It is up to each one of us whether they indeed become gravestones and mausoleums for a God we suspect may be dead, or whether instead they will be places for a saving encounter with the triune God, places of consolation and power from on high, places where we Christians experience one another simultaneously as brothers and sisters of the one Lord in concrete acts of love.

MEDITATION

Father in heaven,
source of holiness and true purpose,
it is right that we praise and glorify your name.
For today we come before you,
to dedicate to your lasting service

this house of prayer, this temple of worship,
this home in which we are nourished by your word and your
      sacraments.
Here is reflected the mystery of the Church.
The Church is fruitful,
made holy by the blood of Christ:
a bride made radiant with his glory,
a virgin splendid in the wholeness of her faith,
a mother blessed through the power of the Spirit.
The Church is holy,
your chosen vineyard: its branches envelop the world,
its tendrils, carried on the tree of the cross,
reach up to the kingdom of heaven.
The Church is favored, the dwelling place of God on earth:
a temple built of living stones,
founded on the apostles
with Jesus Christ its corner stone.
The Church is exalted,
a city set on a mountain:
a beacon to the whole world,
bright with the glory of the Lamb,
and echoing the prayers of her saints.
Lord,
send your Spirit from heaven
to make this church an ever-holy place,
and this altar a ready table for the sacrifice of Christ.
Here may the waters of baptism
overwhelm the shame of sin;
here may your people die to sin
and live again through grace as your children.
Here may your children,
gathered around your altar,
celebrate the memorial of the Paschal Lamb,
and be fed at the table
of Christ's word and Christ's body.
Here may prayer, the Church's banquet,
resound through heaven and earth
as a plea for the world's salvation.
Here may the poor find justice,
the victims of oppression, true freedom.
From here may the whole world
clothed in the dignity of the children of God,
enter with gladness your city of peace.

We ask this through our Lord Jesus Christ, your Son,
who lives and reigns with you and the Holy Spirit,
one God, for ever and ever. Amen.

Prayer for the Dedication of a Church [12]

Christ the King

LITURGICAL GUIDE

In the year 325 the first ecumenical council took place in Nicea in Asia Minor. At that council Christ's full divinity was clearly defined in opposition to the heresy of Arius: Christ is "God from God, light from light, true God from true God . . . of one being with the Father." Sixteen hundred years later, in 1925, Pope Pius XI proclaimed that the most effective means of protection from the destructive powers of the time was the recognition of Christ's kingship. He thought this could be most effectively reinforced by the introduction of a special feast for Christ the King: "For solemnities are more efficacious than any document coming from the Church's magisterium, because they instruct all the faithful not only once, but every year, and reach not only the mind but the heart" (encyclical *Quas primas*, December 11, 1925). Here he referred to the idea behind the celebration, which also comes to direct expression on other days in the liturgical year (e.g., Epiphany, Easter, the Ascension). The original date (the Sunday before All Saints) was fortunately transferred by the new General Norms of 1969 to the last Sunday of the Church year, whereby it becomes clear that Jesus Christ, as our risen Lord and king, is the goal of our earthly pilgrimage and the means to eternal happiness.

The Mass for this feast has different scriptural readings, including the responsorial psalm, in each of the three annual cycles. The use of this richer biblical deposit makes it possible to give a more comprehensive portrait of Christ. This can be demonstrated by a brief examination of the Gospels.

In year A we encounter the majestic judge of the world who passes sentence according to how we have demonstrated, or failed to demonstrate, our love for our neighbor (Matt 25:31-37). In year B we see how Jesus acknowledges his royal status before Pilate, although his kingdom is not of this world (John 18:33-37). In year C the Gospel makes clear that, even in the humiliation of his passion, Jesus still possesses the royal power to lead people into his glory (Luke 23:35-43).

As for those parts of the Mass that remain the same, the opening verse presents the content of the paschal mystery in powerful brevity: the lamb who was slain has received strength, divinity, wisdom, power, and honor (Rev 5:12; 1:6). Christ is the king of creation (opening prayer), for whom the alleluia verse rejoices with the same words that, on Palm Sunday, the crowds called out to him (Mark 11:9). We ask that Christ's sacrifice bestow on all people unity and peace (prayer over the gifts). The special Preface praises Christ as the eternal high priest and universal king who at the end of time will hand over to his Father the kingdom of truth and life, of holiness and grace, of justice, love, and peace. The communion verse and the concluding prayer petition peace and a share in Christ's eternal kingship.

SPIRITUAL REFLECTION

On the final Sunday of the Church year the liturgy shows us the origin and the goal of our faith: Jesus Christ, the ruler of the world. Since Christian antiquity we have celebrated him in the Gloria thus: "you alone are the Holy One, you alone are the Lord, you alone are the Most High." That is a kind of explanation of what is meant by the title "Christ the King." Even if the term "king" seems to some a bit dated, the content retains its validity, then as now. Christ himself declared solemnly, in a situation where it was a matter of life or death, that is, when being examined by Pilate: "I am a king" (John 18:37).

At the same time he made clear on this and other occasions that his kingdom was not of this world. In contrast to the rulers of this world he has no desire to dominate others, but rather to serve, and to give his life for the salvation of the world (cf. Matt 20:25-28). Correspondingly, his kingdom, which he will establish and lead, also has a different style of government than the kingdoms and nation states of this world. What the New Testament has to say about this is crystallized by the special Preface into seven distinct concepts: a kingdom of truth and life, of holiness and grace, of justice, love, and peace. Each of these titles unfolds into an entire program by itself.

Kingdom of Truth

Truth is the agreement of our understanding and life with reality as God sees it. Christ has brought us this truth; indeed, he describes it as one of the purposes of his incarnation, as he says to Pilate: "For this I was born, and for this I came into the world, to testify to the truth" (John 18:37). In the revelation and direction he gives there is no deception or lie, no error or confusion.

Kingdom of Life

Christ desires to help people to lead worthwhile lives, capable of passing over into an unending, eternal life. Thus he can proclaim as the meaning and goal of his coming "I came that they may have life, and have it abundantly" (John 10:10).

Kingdom of Salvation and Grace

Jesus would like to lead all people to freedom from guilt and entanglement with evil through the forgiving love of God, and to participation in God's simplicity and majesty, the "source of all holiness." This kind of perfection is not possible through one's own powers, but only through the helping and "sanctifying" grace of God. God it is who, through Christ and the Holy Spirit, makes possible such a desire and its fulfillment.

Kingdom of Justice

In the last analysis all justice is the judgment of humanity according to God's will. When will the kingdom of justice be realized? Only when for all—as for Jesus—it is food and drink to do the will of their heavenly Father in every sphere of life (cf. John 4:34). Just how important it is to Jesus that a person regard this as a lifelong effort is shown by the fact that he made it the object of the third petition in the Lord's Prayer.

Kingdom of Love

The obligation to love God and neighbor runs like a scarlet thread through the entire New Testament. Jesus emphasizes the achievement of this love as the central commandment, the bond of all perfection. In the realm of such love, egoism of any sort has no place; here reigns only selfless, heartfelt and active love for God and our fellow human beings. The standard of such love is Jesus' love for us: "Just as I have loved you, you also should love one another" (John 13:34).

Kingdom of Freedom

On many occasions Jesus blessed his disciples, saying "peace be with you!" He described peace as the great gift to his disciples: "peace I leave with you; my peace I give to you;" however, he immediately added the clarification: "I do not give to you as the world gives" (John 14:27). The Hebrew and Aramaic word *shalom* is much more comprehensive than our English word "peace." It means the condition of being in a proper relation and harmony with God and our fellow human beings; it is a characteristic of messianic salvation.

Could not the realization of this reign of Christ with its seven aspects already create on earth a condition of the greatest possible happiness in which discord and war, hatred and jealousy would be outlawed, in which one person would not only put up with another, but in loving concern help others to bear their difficulties; in which, in spite of the transitory and passing nature of everything earthly, humankind would be marked by harmony both within and without and possessed by the same striving and the same hope, because God is all in all?

It is just such a kingdom that Christ means to erect. All of us are called to help him in this project. His gifts are our tasks. We are given the opportunity, through patient effort, to become ever more conformed to his image. The service of God, of the neighbor, and of the world are the spheres in which Christ's kingdom will be built. That in this we always fall short of the ideal is our own fault. It is, however, the appeal of the feast of Christ the King, and our enduring obligation, to take up this project ever anew.

MEDITATION

O Christ, Master of heaven and earth,
Lord of powers, dominations, and thrones.
You are the first and you are the last,
Beginning and end.

In your hands rests the fate of humanity.
Nothing on earth can escape your power.
You pass judgment over all peoples,
Rich in mercy.

Empires rise, bloom, and fade away,
but yours outlasts them all,
For your lordship is bestowed by God,
Its source is everlasting.

None of the great ones can measure themselves against you;
Lord of lords, king of all ages,
Brilliance of the Father, mirror of divine majesty,
Enthroned in heaven.

To you be the glory, to you and to the Father,
and also to the Spirit may praise be sung.
To God, the three in one, praise, honor, and glory
now and forever. Amen.

Vesper hymn for the feast of Christ the King
(from the German Breviary)

Source Notes, Part 4

1. Pius Parsch, *The Church's Year of Grace* (Collegeville: The Liturgical Press, 1962) 1.375.

2. Bernard of Clairvaux, *Homélie à la louange de la Vierge Marie* 4:8-9, quoted in Robert Gantoy and Romain Swaeles, eds., *Days of the Lord* 1, translated by Gregory LaNave and Donald Molloy (Collegeville: The Liturgical Press, 1991) 174.

3. Karl Rahner, *Gebete des Lebens* (8th ed. Freiburg: Herder, 1989) 174.

4. Declaration of ten Christian denominations, Pentecost 1991.

5. Friedrich Wilhelm Weber, *Dreizehnlinden* (1878) in Reinhard Hörmann, "Reflexionen über das Verhältnis Friedrich Wilhelm Webers zur Religion" in *Friedrich Wilhelm Weber. Arzt – Politiker – Dichter* (Paderborn: Bonifatius Druck-Buch-Verlag, 1994) 188.

6. *The Hymnal 1982*, no. 320.

7. Theodor Schneider, *Gewandeltes Eucharistieverständnis* (Zürich: Benziger, 1969) 37ff.

8. *Gotteslob*, 780.

9. Sabine Naegeli, *Du hast mein Dunkel geteilt* (9th ed. Freiburg: Herder, 1990) 106.

10. Christian Morgenstern, "Das Kreuz," in idem, *Gesammelte Werke* (Munich: R. Piper & Co., 1965) 171 (there untitled).

11. *The Hymnal 1982*, no. 162.

12. *The Rites of the Catholic Church* (Collegeville: The Liturgical Press, 1991) 2.378–79.

A Selection from the
Proper of the Saints

of protecting Mary and Jesus. In the Old Testament reading from the second book of Samuel, God promises King David that his throne will endure forever, a promise that is fulfilled in the messianic kingdom of Jesus. The link between David and Jesus is "Joseph, the husband of Mary," who according to the Gospel descends from the house of David (cf. Matt 1:16; Luke 1:27; 2:4). The responsorial psalm (Psalm 89) meditates on this promise. The New Testament reading (Rom 4:13, 16-18, 22) praises the faith of Abraham. Like him, Joseph was also ready to believe and obey God's word.

In the Gospel for this feast (Matt 1:16, 18-21, 24a) Joseph learns from the "angel of the Lord [who] appeared in a dream" of the mystery that the woman he is engaged to is to become the mother of God. At God's behest he contracts a marriage with her according to the Law and later gives the child the name Jesus ("YHWH helps"). Thereby Joseph is seen before the Law as Jesus' father. Instead of this Gospel the pericope about the twelve-year-old Jesus in the Temple (Luke 2:41-51a) may be chosen. The intentions of the presider's prayers are that the Church may "continue to serve its Lord" (opening prayer), serve God with a pure heart (prayer over the gifts), and secure God's protection (concluding prayer).

SPIRITUAL REFLECTION

The more brightly the sun shines, the more effectively it blots out the stars. Does this not hold true also of Joseph, the carpenter from Nazareth, the "husband of Mary, the mother of God," as the Missal calls him?

More than eleven hundred years elapsed before he received his own liturgical feast in the Western Church, and before the first church was erected in his honor. Of course it is proper that Jesus as the sun of holiness stands in the center of pious devotion, and his mother as well, who through her "yes" to becoming the mother of God and through her maternal service for the salvation of the world and our salvation also has earned a high and well-deserved place in our grateful remembrance. These brightly illumined figures, however, allow Joseph, "the husband of Mary" (Matt 1:16) and the foster father of Jesus, to retreat into the background of our attention and veneration. This is apparent already with the evangelists, who have not passed on to us even a single one of Joseph's words.

At the same time, the little that the gospels do report to us about him qualifies him eminently to be recognized and esteemed as a great saint and a commendable collaborator in the history of salvation. For this we do not have to rely on the more or less legendary pious stories that grew up around the second century in the so-called apocryphal literature, the products of an unbridled imagination.

One characteristic that the New Testament expressly attributes to Joseph is his righteousness (Matt 1:19). Today's special Preface also mentions and praises this virtue. A righteous person, as this term was used of the ancestors in the Old Testament, is one who determines what to do and not to do according to God's will. This was also the case with Joseph. God's will was the compass according to which he oriented himself in all matters. Whenever and wherever the will of God became clear to him, he obeyed it without hesitation.

Scripture reports three revelations of God's will that were given to Joseph through "an angel of the Lord in a dream": The first reached him as he was wrestling with the thought that he should quietly divorce Mary, his betrothed, who according to the current custom and law was still living with her parents and yet was already promised to him. For the child that she was expecting was not his. Then God's message reached him: "Joseph, son of David, have no fear about taking Mary as your wife. It is by the Holy Spirit that she has conceived this child" (Matt 1:20). Joseph believes and obeys.

The second revelation of God's will breaks unexpectedly into Joseph's life just as he has bidden farewell to the wise men from the East: "Get up, take the child and his mother, and flee to Egypt. Stay there until I tell you otherwise. Herod is searching for the child to destroy him" (Matt 2:13). Joseph believes and obeys, accepting the difficult plight of an exile and refugee.

After the death of the child-murderer Herod the third message reaches him: "Get up, take the child and his mother, and set out for the land of Israel. Those who had designs on the life of the child are dead" (Matt 2:20). Joseph believes and obeys.

Most probably the words of the prophet Samuel were familiar to him from the synagogue service: "Surely, to obey is better than sacrifice" (1 Sam 15:22). To listen and obey when God speaks and commands: this was Joseph's righteousness, a quality that marked him also in all the other areas of his life. From this basic attitude we may with justice deduce that he also carried out his daily labor, through which he provided a home for the "holy family," with this same quiet readiness. Certainly he was for the growing Jesus the living example of the dignity of service, recorded in Jesus' saying: "Whoever wishes to be great among you must be your servant" (Matt 20:26). Where the love of God and humanity is joined with such service, the service of neighbor becomes the service of God. In this connection we do not

When Jesus himself comes down to the Jordan to let himself be baptized by him, John utters those words that have been taken up into the eucharistic liturgy: "Here is the Lamb of God who takes away the sin of the world! This is he of whom I said, 'After me comes a man who ranks ahead of me because he was before me.' . . . this is the Son of God" (John 1:29-34).

Selflessly, he leads his own disciples to Jesus (John 1:35-37). He experiences no jealousy when people tell him that Jesus is also baptizing and is attracting more people than himself. For he describes himself as "the friend of the bridegroom," not as his rival. "He must increase, but I must decrease" (John 3:22-30). This attitude by the Baptist must have particularly impressed the painter Matthias Grünewald (Mathis Nithart) when he created the famous depiction of the crucifixion for the Isenheimer altar: while Jesus' mother, John the apostle, and Mary Magdalene stand to the right of the crucified in the deepest sorrow or kneel at the foot of the cross, John the Baptist, wearing a hair shirt, stands to the left as seen from Jesus on the cross, a lamb at his feet, and points with an exaggeratedly long index finger toward Christ, as if he wished to underline the words of the scriptural quotation given below: "He must increase, but I must decrease."

John's service as the one who prepares the way for the Messiah is supported and strengthened in its credibility by his personal purity and magnanimity of character. There is no trace of self-interest, moodiness, or indolence in him. He continues to lead his life of privation in the wilderness, apparent in his food and clothing: a robe of camel hair with a leather belt; locusts and wild honey, and no alcoholic drink (cf. Luke 7:33). Elegant clothing and an opulent lifestyle are foreign to him. He is no reed that is blown by the wind, as Jesus himself says of him (Luke 7:24). He does not pay attention to public opinion, but feels himself obliged only by the truth. Even before the mighty he shows himself unafraid and exposes their faults and crimes. With courage he opposes the Pharisees and Sadducees and a criminal military occupation, and does not even cower before the palace of Herod. This devotion to God's truth and justice leads ultimately to his arrest and his martyr's death, after he had denounced Herod's adulterous behavior with his brother's wife. Is it possible that even in those days there were some people who wanted to detract from such a martyrdom by saying "he should have kept his mouth shut"?

From a view of John's important service for salvation and breadth of character we can understand why already the ancient Church gave particular veneration to the Baptist. Just as once Moses, after the terrible punishment of wandering in the wilderness, saw the promised land from afar but could not enter it, so also John the Baptist stands on the border between the old and the new covenants. He was fated to expend all his strength to prepare for the latter, but himself not to live in it.

MEDITATION

You served Christ the Lord as herald.
Eternal decrees found in you their messenger.
Happily we all praise your name:
We hail you, John.

The mother still carries you in her womb,
but you already feel the king draw near;
Joy moves you, impels you to greet him
before even he is born.

You choose desert and wilderness as your abode,
You proclaim the arrival of the longed-for Savior,
You preach conversion, call the people to repentance,
so that all may be ready.

He whom the prophets once promised as the light
that they saw from a distance, only intimating,
the one who takes away all the sins of the world,
you call by name.

Voice of one calling, who makes straight the path,
the Lord has chosen you above all others:
Jesus, the Savior, allows himself to be baptized by you,
he, the Lamb of God.

Praise and honor to God, the eternal Father,
Honor to the Son, whom you announced to us,
Honor to the Spirit, who witnessed him to you,
now and forever. Amen.

Vesper Hymn for the Feast
(from the German breviary)

attack of forces hostile to God against the Church will not be success-ful. The Church of Christ—for he, not Peter, is indeed the Lord of the Church—will successfully withstand any attempt to destroy it, whether through material forms of power or ideological attack. "From this we can also conclude that the promise cannot be limited to the per-son of Peter; it necessarily includes all of his successors in the position of primate."[9]

In what follows, Christ employs a new image, promising Peter the "keys of the kingdom of heaven." The power of the keys symbolizes complete power in a house, which belongs primarily to the owner of the house, but may be assigned to an administrator as the owner's rep-resentative. This is exactly what Jesus had done to Peter with respect to his Church. This fullness of power consists in the ability to bind and loose. According to the linguistic conventions of the time, this be-tokens the power to forbid or permit, to place under a ban and release from a ban, to condemn and to set free. There are good reasons why many exegetes discern also in this image an indication of the offices of leading and shepherding that were entrusted to Peter in a special way. His pronouncements and dispositions (and those of his successors) are also valid in God's eyes. In this way great power was entrusted to a weak man, power that he as a "good and trustworthy slave" was, of course, to use in the spirit of his Lord.

While Peter's apostolic activity after Christ's resurrection and as-cension and after the sending of the Holy Spirit was directed primar-ily to the Jewish Christian communities, the divine call led Paul into the Gentile missions. The Preface for this feast summarizes the differ-ences and similarities of these two leading apostles in a few telling lines: "Peter raised up the Church from the faithful flock of Israel. Paul brought your call to the nations, and became the teacher of the world. Each in his chosen way gathered into unity the one family of Christ. Both shared a martyr's death and are praised throughout the world."

The grace of deep insight transformed Paul into an outstanding teacher and preacher of the mystery of Christ, our "life in Christ" about which 2 Cor 5:17 says: "so if anyone is in Christ, there is a new creation: everything old has passed away; see, everything has become new!" What Paul accomplished in his missionary labors among the Gentiles is truly amazing and can only be explained, as he himself em-phasizes on many occasions, through God's power accompanying and leading him. "I can do all things through him who strengthens me" (Phil 4:13). It is distressing to read his listing of all the sufferings and tribulations he had endured as an apostle (2 Cor 11:23-33). The former persecutor of Christians has been transformed into a witness to Christ who was even ready to face death. Thus the second reading of the Mass can place precisely those words in his mouth that resound like a testament at the conclusion of his life: "I . . . am already being poured out like a libation. The time of my dissolution is near. I have fought the good fight, I have finished the race, I have kept the faith. From now on a merited crown awaits me; on that Day the Lord, just judge that he is, will award it to me—and not only to me but to all who have looked for his appearing with eager longing" (2 Tim 4:6-8).

These two apostles merit our grateful remembrance because of their fidelity to their calling and their service for Christ's Church even to death. At the same time they are shining examples and models for all those who love Christ and his church and through baptism and confirmation share in an apostolic calling, in the labor for God's reign and in "hoping against hope" (cf. Rom 4:18).

MEDITATION

To the martyr's death of these apostles
this holy day is dedicated,
Triumph and crowns today adorn
Saints Peter and Paul together.

The blood of their heroic deaths
unites these two equals;
they who followed their Lord and God
today receive the crown of faith.

The first disciple called was Peter,
still in grace is Paul his equal,
a holy vessel for the Lord, and
as strong in faith as Saint Peter.

By having his cross turned upside down
Simon leaves to God alone the honor;
he is to be raised up, and he remembers
what Christ prophesied for him.

When he becomes old, as was said to him,
he will be girded with a rope, get up
and go where he would not
to die willingly a bitter death.

nacle of the Lord would be stained with sin. Thus arose the belief in
Mary's freedom from original sin and her protection from every kind
of personal sin. However, since death and the decay of the human
body are the consequences of sin it did not seem proper that the sin-
less virgin Mary would be subjected to this law of mortality.

The arguments from appropriateness, which have their roots in
Scripture, were presented in detail in the apostolic constitution
Munificentissimus Deus on November 1, 1950, which said that the new
dogma rested primarily upon the faith of the Church, "since the universal Church, within which dwells the Spirit of Truth who infallibly
directs it towards an ever more perfect knowledge of the revealed
truths, has expressed its own belief [in the truth of Mary's assump-
tion] many times over the course of the centuries." This conviction
was made public in numerous statements from the sixth century onward and by the celebration of the feast on August 15 with this emphasis for over twelve centuries, in numerous petitions from bishops
and lay people for an appropriate dogmatic statement, and finally in
the results of a survey of all the bishops of the world conducted in
1946. At that time "the Bishops of the entire world . . . almost unani-
mously petitioned that the truth of the bodily Assumption of the
Blessed Virgin Mary into heaven should be defined as a dogma of divine and Catholic faith."

What, however, can such a dogmatic statement mean for us contemporary Christians? In a century that has suffered two world wars
and numerous other conflicts with millions of deaths and the destruction of human life, with genocide and persecutions driving people
from their ancestral homes, this dogma is a promise and consoling vision of the fullness of salvation that is intended for each person. "It is
as if in Mary, the one fully redeemed, we had already dropped anchor
in the kingdom of perfection to which now our hope for salvation may
be attached anew."[10] Mary's destiny is inextricably bound up with that
of Jesus in both joy and sorrow; her body was conformed to the transfigured body of Christ. This will also be the destiny of all those who
have joined themselves to Jesus in faith and love. Wherever this meaning of the dogma is accepted and endorsed, it is enough to produce
confidence and the strength to endure the strains and sufferings of
both body and soul, and to impart a deep-rooted joy that cannot be destroyed by suffering.

It is thus understandable that the Preface for this feast calls us to
give thanks and to praise God for this work of divine grace. Because
full salvation has been realized in Mary, she has become "the beginning and the pattern of the Church in its perfection, and a sign of hope
and comfort for your people on their pilgrim way." This thought is

also expressed in the opening prayer. We can thus understand why in Catholic lands this Marian feast enjoys great prestige and is celebrated with special solemnity.

MEDITATION

Today goes to rest the holy, living shrine of the living God, who took the Creator himself into herself, into the temple of the Lord that no human hand had built for him. Today the heavenly Eden of the new Adam receives a living paradise in which the judgment of banishment has been rescinded, in which the tree of life has been planted. Today the pure virgin—a living heaven—was received into the tents of heaven . . . How could the underworld have received her, how could decay have overcome her body, in which Life itself had lived? No, a more direct and straighter, easier path to heaven was opened to her. When Christ, who is the way, the truth, and the life, can say "where I am, there also will my servant be," how much more must not his mother be there as well!

John Damascene (d. 750) [11]

The Birthday of the Blessed Virgin Mary
(September 8)

LITURGICAL GUIDE

In the celebration of Mary's birth we encounter one of the oldest Marian feasts. Its origin lies most probably in the consecration of a Marian church in Jerusalem near the pool at the sheep gate (cf. John 5:2) on September 8 some time in the fifth century. The house in which Mary was born is also supposed to have been close to this pool. The later church of St. Anne took over this tradition.

From the hymns of the Greek deacon Romanos, who was active in Constantinople around the year 500, we may conclude that this Marian feast was already deeply rooted among the people. It can be shown to have existed in Rome in the seventh century and it was embellished by

Pope Sergius I (687–701) with a procession from the church of Hadrian in the Forum to the church of Santa Maria Maggiore. After the feasts of the birth of the Lord and of his precursor John the Baptist, it is the third birthday celebration in the Roman calendar.

The Mass of the feast, like the office of the day, is marked by great joy (cf. opening verse, responsorial psalm, and concluding prayer). It celebrates Mary's birth with a view primarily to her status as the mother of God. This is true of the opening verse, the opening prayer and prayer over the gifts, the alleluia, and the communion verse. The concluding prayer names Mary the bringer of "the dawn of hope and salvation to the world." The special Preface praises her election and blessing "above all women" and emphasizes her importance in the events of salvation: "In her the dawn of salvation shines forth. She gave birth to Christ, the sun of our salvation." The Gospel for the day recites the genealogy of Jesus (Matt 1:1-16) and the revelation concerning the Spirit's role in Mary's motherhood as this was shared with Joseph (Matt 1:18-23). The Old Testament reading from the book of Micah (Mic 5:1-4a) contains the promise to Bethlehem that from it the new ruler of Israel would come forth, the shepherd with the power of the Lord: "He shall be the one of peace." Romans 8:28-30 may be taken as an alternative reading. There the subject is our eternal vocation and salvation.

Spiritual Reflection

In contrast to the birthdays of the Lord and his precursor John, the New Testament gives no details about Mary's birth. Not even the names of her parents are mentioned. Only the *Protoevangelium of James,* an apocryphal writing from the second century (many parts substantially later), gives the names Joachim and Anne and reports several legends concerning Mary's childhood, most of which should be rejected as fables. In the gospels themselves we encounter Mary as the virgin of Nazareth for the first time at the scene of the annunciation. This reports only the information about her that is important for the Christ event and for our salvation.

The primary event in Mary's life is the moment of the annunciation. God's eternal wisdom had chosen her to be the mother of God's Son. By her free assent the "servant of the Lord" activated this election and thereby made a contribution to salvation founded on God's respect for human freedom. In this sense Bishop Irenaeus of Lyons (d. ca. 202) could already write that Mary "by yielding obedience" became "the cause of salvation both to herself and the whole human race" and that "the knot of Eve's disobedience was loosed by the obedience of Mary."[12] Without diminishing the sole intercessory role of the unique Savior, Jesus Christ (cf. 1 Tim 2:5-6) one must concede that in the history of salvation Mary's contribution was decisive, in that, by her "yes," she opened the gate for the coming of the Savior.

After this crucial moment in her own and in all our lives she continued to remain the faithful servant of the Lord. Accompanying her Son along his path proved to be no triumphal march, but had to be carried out in faith, service, and suffering. She withstood these tests, and it is the highest recognition and confirmation of her service in the work of salvation that her Son, as he hung upon the cross, entrusted her to John and through him to us all as our mother. Her physical motherhood of Jesus was, as it were, broadened into a spiritual motherhood for the Church. This became visible when she prayed for the descent of the Holy Spirit in the midst of the assembled disciples (cf. Acts 1:14). Where before she dedicated herself to her physical Son as mother and servant, henceforth her loving concern and intercession are offered on behalf of the mystical body of Christ, the Church. Therefore the Second Vatican Council proclaims that "by her maternal charity, Mary cares for the brethren of her Son who still journey on earth surrounded by dangers and difficulties, until they are led to their happy fatherland."[13]

The Church itself looks up to Mary with grateful love. As both the first and most perfect recipient of salvation, she brings "the dawn of hope and salvation to the world," as the concluding prayer for this feast and many other witnesses attest. The Church sees in her both an example and a model for Christian life, since she "shines forth to the whole community of the elect as a model of the virtues."[14] She serves as a practical model for each one of us in her unconditioned faith in God's word and in her willing obedience, in her preserving and turning over in her thoughts the divine words and actions, in her day-to-day love of neighbor, shown by her visit to her cousin Elizabeth and at the marriage feast of Cana. She is also a model of trust in God's guidance even in her darkest moments, and through her steadfastness in suffering displayed during her Son's passion.

We thus understand why through all the centuries the Church has continually turned toward its heavenly mother in grateful and reverent love. It does so through the celebration of numerous feast days and memorials, in the special intentions during the two Marian months of May and October, in countless prayers and songs, hymns, and musical compositions, in masterpieces of painting and sculpture, in the dedication of cathedrals, churches, and shrines, in Marian pilgrimages and processions, and in a variety of devotional customs. This veneration of

Mary does not lead us away from Christ, but rather closer to him. A person who is close to Mary is automatically close to Christ, and vice versa: a person who is close to Christ automatically loves and venerates his mother. "As our sister in the faith, she is a valuable companion to each one of us on our unique journey of faith. . . . If we could all take her more fully as a model our society, and indeed our Church would certainly be more attractive."[15]

MEDITATION

Christians have always found in Mary a figure of consolation, of encouragement, and of hope springing anew. What draws us so powerfully to her is the liberating energy of grace. In the Greek language this is immediately apparent, for *charis* means favor as well as loveliness, charm, and beauty. Mary immaculate is the perfection of the "charming" woman. She lives in an interior self-sufficiency and shines forth as a counter-image to the discounted, displaced, and discouraged people of today. In her freedom she takes the risk of abandoning herself to the transcendent God, to whom indeed she hands herself over for better or for worse. She falls completely into God's hands, but this God catches her and raises her up from death into his love. Therefore all Christians may risk the adventure of grace without reservation.

Wolfgang Beinert[16]

All Saints
(November 1)

LITURGICAL GUIDE

One can detect the beginnings of veneration of the saints by the middle of the second century. The martyrs were the first to be so honored, and very soon the apostles were equated with them in liturgical observance as public witnesses to the faith. Special veneration was then also extended to those who had suffered imprisonment, torture, or exile for the sake of the faith ("confessors"). After the great persecutions of the Roman empire, honor was gradually accorded to outstanding bishops like Martin of Tours and also to ascetics and virgins who had distinguished themselves by extraordinary Christian discipleship and whose lives were viewed as a kind of unbloody martyrdom.

In order to check an uncontrolled expansion of the veneration of saints, the Church set up a formal procedure for canonization even before the end of the first millennium. Later the criteria were made progressively more rigorous, so that heroic Christian discipleship was required, as well as proof of miracles obtained by calling upon that person.

The origins of the feast of All Saints lie in the East, where as early as the fourth century there was a memorial for all the martyrs; this was celebrated in different places on three different dates: in Rome on May 13, in England and Ireland in the eighth century on November 1. In the ninth century this date was accepted in Rome and the other regions. In the reform of the rubrics in 1955 under Pius XII the vigil and octave were removed.

The Mass for the feast in the new Missal has taken over the earlier readings, enriched by a second reading and a special Preface. The Preface is virtually a hymn to the mystery of this celebration. The first reading (Rev 7:2-4, 9, 14) describes the saints as the "one hundred and forty-four thousand from every tribe of Israel" and as the "huge crowd . . . from every nation, race, people, and tongue," who stand before the throne and the Lamb wearing white garments and with palm branches in their hands. The second reading sees the gift of becoming God's children as the foundation of our final glory. While in the alleluia verse Jesus invites all those who labor and are burdened to receive rest from him (Matt 11:28), the Gospel with the beatitudes from the Sermon on the Mount (Matt 5:1-12a) points out the way to holiness and perfection. The communion verse includes three of these blessings. In the presider's prayers we place our trust in the intercession of so many saints (opening prayer and prayer over the gifts) and ask for the Holy Spirit's guidance along the pilgrim way toward the eternal banquet.

SPIRITUAL REFLECTION

As the liturgical year nears its end the Church looks in a special way toward those of its members who have already stepped through the portals of death and enjoy eternal fulfillment. It is of them that Revelation says: "See, the home of God is among mortals. He will dwell with them as their God; they will be his peoples, and God himself will be with them; he will wipe every tear from their eyes. Death will be no more; mourning and crying and pain will be no more, for the first things have passed away" (Rev 21:3-4).

One could call the feast of All Saints a harvest celebration for the fruit of the paschal mystery, for the saints are indeed the fruit of God's victorious grace, a joyous ode to the divine plan of salvation and Christ's saving grace. The words of Matthias Claudius (1740–1815) "We plow the fields and scatter the seed upon the land, but all its growth and increase lies in heaven's hand" also hold true for all the saints. On the one hand "heaven" never simply falls into one's lap without great efforts over a long period of time, just as a farmer must sow and harvest, or as a runner in a race must go all out to win the prize (cf. 1 Cor 9:24-25). Indeed, Jesus himself demands of his disciples wakefulness, self-conquest, and prayer if they are not to fall short of their goal. The latter is not reached through pious words alone. "Not everyone who says to me, 'Lord, Lord,' will enter the kingdom of heaven, but only the one who does the will of my Father in heaven" (Matt 7:21). On the other hand, for every good work a person requires God's anticipating and helping grace: "growth and increase lie in heaven's hand." To that extent every successful Christian life is the fruit of a mysterious cooperation between human effort and divine grace.

This kind of insight forbids any self-preening. "What do you have that you did not receive? And if you received it, why do you boast as if it were not a gift?" (1 Cor 4:7). This is true also and especially for those extraordinary qualities of life we call holiness and about which the second Eucharistic Prayer says that God is their source. To clarify this through a comparison, whoever enjoys the moon's light is actually enjoying the sun's light, for the former is only the reflected light of the sun. The sun of the saints is the triune God and all the light of the saints is only a reflection of the light of divine grace.

The Preface for this feast makes it clear that the saints in heaven include not only those who because of their heroic love of God and neighbor have been canonized through a public process, but also all "our brothers and sisters . . . [who] sing [God's] praise forever." What is to prevent us from seeing among them the many of our loved ones who were close to us in life and who walked firmly and courageously along the path of Christian discipleship? If we take seriously the promise of "sanctifying grace," then these also are part of the heavenly company of the saints, even if no spectacular miracles have so far taken place through their intercession. But from this it follows that we are close to them in the medium of the divine love that encompasses all things, and that we may converse with them and ask them to intercede for us, even if this is only allowed in the private sphere. In this sense the feast of All Saints can take on a personal character, a markedly familiar aspect.

The Christian teaching about heavenly perfection and the counsel that recurs again and again in Scripture that we should never lose sight of our goal should not be misunderstood as a dispensation from our obligation to take seriously the shaping of this world. In this matter as in others one must beware of a false "either-or." Certainly there have been times and people that in their concern for an otherworldly paradise have scarcely taken notice of the proper order of this world. This is an improper attitude, but in our time we are threatened by the opposite extreme, the danger that in concentrating exclusively on earthly goals and projects we may lose sight of any transcendence. Here the inclusive, catholic "et–et," "both–and" allows us to discover a golden mean. Anyone who neglects to feel concern and to labor for a better world in the name of a "one-sided longing for paradise" is not acting in the spirit of Christ. Such a one is flouting the principal commandment of love of neighbor, which obliges us to struggle for peace, justice, protection of the environment, and the prosperity of humankind. As Walbert Bühlmann once said, we can only make the hope of heaven credible to our fellow human beings if we bring a little more of heaven down to earth. Both the beatitudes of the Sermon on the Mount (Matt 5:3-12) and Jesus' speech about the last judgment (Matt 25:31-46) obligate us to do this, without losing sight of the final goal God intended, our eternal happiness.

MEDITATION

The Church can only go out to meet its approaching Lord and place its hope in him if it becomes a witness of his presence for others. In the words of Dietrich Bonhoeffer, it can only be Church if it wills to be a Church for others (for the world) . . .

Those who lead their lives as followers of Christ concern themselves also with the physical and spiritual state of their neighbors. They work for a humanly worthy life for others, with food, clothing, shelter, and education in a social context of political and social justice (cf. Matt 25:31-46). They are concerned about everyone in the human race, not only those who share their beliefs (Gal 6:10). Christian faith has an obvious political and social dimension even though its political function is not to make itself its own raison d'être. It is only in doing good, moreover, that Christians, with their eyes on the Lord who is approaching, achieve the righteousness, the ultimate communion of love with Christ and the Father that gives eternal life (Matt 25:46).

Gerhard Ludwig Müller [17]

The Commemoration of All the Faithful Departed (All Souls) (November 2)

LITURGICAL GUIDE

This commemoration of all the faithful departed, as it is officially called in the Roman calendar, is a liturgical memorial of a special sort. It is not a solemnity, but it is included among the optional memorials in the proper of the saints. As early as the second century we have testimonies that during their eucharistic celebrations Christians prayed for their dead. Initially the third day after burial and the anniversary of the death were the preferred occasions. Later the seventh, thirtieth, and fortieth day after burial were added to this list. The specific feast of All Souls originated in 998, when abbot Odilo of Cluny (994–1048) instituted this memorial on November 2 for all the monasteries under his jurisdiction. It quickly spread throughout the entire Western Church.

The custom that on this day each priest could celebrate three Masses developed first in the fifteenth century among the Dominicans in Valencia (Spain), and was quickly imitated in many other countries. Pope Benedict XV extended this privilege to all priests in 1915, with the condition that they could accept a stipend only for one Mass. For Germany there exists a papal indult permitting a stipend for a second or third Mass, but it must be turned over to the St. Boniface Society for the benefit of the diaspora. There is no obligation to take advantage of this privilege to celebrate three Masses. Should the feast of All Souls fall on a Sunday, the Mass of All Souls is celebrated, but the office of the day is that of Sunday.

Masses for the dead have been greatly enhanced by the provision of four new Prefaces. Their clear intention is to give expression to the "paschal character of Christian death"[18] and to proclaim the paschal mystery as the foundation of our hope. For this reason the sequence *Dies irae* and other texts in which fear of the final judgment depressed rather than uplifted the faithful have been suppressed. All the texts and readings of the three Masses for All Souls should strengthen our hope in the resurrection.

SPIRITUAL REFLECTION

Human experience can give us no information as to what transpires during and after a person's death. For this we have to fall back on the revelation of sacred Scripture, and the theology and doctrine of the Church drawn from it. The Gospel for the first Mass for All Souls proclaims an important revelation. Here Jesus delivers a revolutionary message about life after death: "I am the resurrection and the life. Those who believe in me, even though they die, will live, and everyone who lives and believes in me will never die" (John 11:25-26). We know from experience the fate of the body: it decays and falls apart. But the body is not the entire person. As Joseph Ratzinger wrote, "what is essential about a human being, the person, remains." The human being as a person is the one who dialogues with God. It is to this one that God has given the divine Word and proclaimed eternal fidelity. It is this one "who even though [he or she dies], will live." God does not permit us to fall; God does not forget us, because God has taken us up in love: "I have written you on the palm of my hand." Because through faith and grace we belong to Christ's mystical body, as human persons we participate in Christ's resurrected body.

It is the Church's teaching that only a person who is in the fullness of God's grace and who has been freed from all sin and the punishment due to sin may participate in the beatific vision. There thus developed the doctrine of a state of purification for those persons who did indeed die in sanctifying grace, but are still burdened with venial sins and "the punishment due to sin" (Karl Rahner). This would be some kind of middle condition that during the Middle Ages received the name "purgatory." The image was often of a place of gruesome torments in which fire played an important role. For this image, reference was made already in the times of the early Christian Fathers to 1 Cor 3:15b. However, given the metaphorical character of that entire section of the letter, this reference is not compelling. Pictures of the fires of purgatory (since the end of the fourteenth century) and supposed apparitions of the "poor souls" amid the flames excited many terrifying visions among Christians during the late Middle Ages and in the following centuries, and encouraged some highly dubious notions. That there cannot be a fire of a physical sort should be obvious from the fact that the human soul (or person) is a spiritual being, and thus cannot be affected by any physical fire or other earthly pain.

If we speak of the "poor souls," we should not overlook the fact that in a certain sense they are also the "rich souls," to the extent that they have died in the grace of justification, sanctifying grace, and for that reason are certain of their eternal happiness with God. What is to be completed for their final perfection through the pains of purification can only take place at the spiritual level. Here a famous phrase from Goethe puts us on the right track: "Only those who have experienced yearning can truly know what I am suffering." The yearning for the beatific vision and union with God may be so burning that it may rightly be compared with the torment of flames, but one should emphasize that this is only a comparison.

We cannot answer questions about the place and manner and length of this purification. Anyone who claims to know more about such matters merits no serious consideration.

It is a defined teaching of the Church that intercessions by the faithful on behalf of these people in the transitional state of purification are both possible and efficacious. The Church's liturgy also takes advantage of this opportunity on various occasions. Thus the Eucharistic Prayer of every Mass contains a "memorial for the dead" in which they are remembered prayerfully: for example, "may these, and all who sleep in Christ, find in your presence light, happiness, and peace" (Eucharistic Prayer 1). Beyond that, the Christians of the early Church already embellished the graves of their dead with a stone on which was carved an intercessory prayer such as "Rest with God" or "Rest in Peace" (*Requiescat in pace* = R.I.P.). In this way a visit to the graves could also strengthen the living in their hope of eternal life.

MEDITATION

That we survive death is an expectation of all peoples and of all religions, and constitutes the core statement of Christianity. Christ is risen; therefore we also will rise one day! It is not that we "must" believe this; rather we "can" believe it and thus be happy, because this belief is also the eternal longing of our hearts.

As to *how* this will take place and how it will be in heaven, this is admittedly a totally different question. About such matters we can only stutter and stammer. There thus only remains for us the hope of being surprised by God's greatness and bigheartedness. We do not need to whisper in God's ear how heaven should be. That could only correspond to our human understanding; the latter, however, is light years below what God has in store. Let us then leave the *how* to God's own care, and let it be God's surprise. We can only say that something is waiting for us that is far more than we could ever expect!

Walbert Bühlmann [19]

Source Notes, Part 5

1. *SC* 103.

2. *LG* 62.

3. Pope Pius IX, bull "Ineffabilis Deus," December 8, 1854.

4. Wolfgang Beinert, "Die mariologischen Dogmen und ihre Entfaltung," in W. Beinert and W. Petri, eds., *Handbuch der Marienkunde* (Regensburg: Pustet, 1984) 289.

5. Bernhard Welte, *Maria, die Mutter Jesu: Meditationen* (5th ed. Freiburg, Basel, and Vienna: Herder, 1980) 45.

6. Ibid., 45–46.

7. Anton Vögtle, "Joseph," in P. Manns, ed., *Die Heiligen* (4th ed. Mainz: Matthias-Grünewald-Verlag, 1979) 8–9.

8. By the author.

9. Karl Staab, *Das Evangelium nach Matthäus. Die Heilige Schrift in deutscher Übersetzung.* Echter Bibel (Würzburg: Echter Verlag, 1958) 91.

10. Leo Scheffczyk in Wolfgang Beinert, ed. *Maria heute ehren* (3rd ed. Freiburg, Basel, and Vienna: Herder, 1979) 142.

11. John Damascene, excerpts from "XV. Augusti. Indormitionem Sanctae dei genitricis Mariae," *Oratio in dormitionem B.M.V. secunda* (2 and 3).

12. *Adv. haer.* 3.22.4. Johannes Quasten, *Patrology* (Westminster, Md.: Christian Classics, 1983) 1.298.

13. *LG* 8.

14. Ibid.

15. Bernhard Welte, *Maria, die Mutter Jesu: Meditationen* (5th ed. Freiburg, Basel, and Vienna: Herder, 1980) 31, 85.

16. From Adam, "Maria, wir rufen zu dir," in W. Beinert and W. Petri, eds. *Handbuch der Marienkunde* 96.

17. Gerhard Ludwig Müller, *Laßt uns mit ihm gehen* (Freiburg: Herder, 1990) 217–18.

18. *SC* 81.

19. Walbert Bühlmann, "Was geschieht im Sterben mit uns," *Dienender Glaube* 65 (1989) 306–307.

INDEX

In this index, when an author is not identified by name in the text itself but only in the corresponding endnote, an asterisk follows the page number.